C. C. L

D1063434

Oceanic Prehistory

Oceanic Prehistory

Richard Shutler, Jr.
University of Iowa

Mary Elizabeth Shutler
San Diego State University

Cummings Publishing Company
Menlo Park, California · Reading, Massachusetts
London · Amsterdam · Don Mills, Ontario · Sydney

This book is in the
Cummings Modular Program in Anthropology

Editorial Board

PAUL T. BAKER
The Pennsylvania State University

JOSEPH B. CASAGRANDE
University of Illinois, Urbana-Champaign

KWANG-CHIH CHANG
Yale University

WARD H. GOODENOUGH
University of Pennsylvania

EUGENE A. HAMMEL
University of California, Berkeley

Copyright ©1975 by Cummings Publishing Company, Inc.
Philippines copyright 1975.

All rights reserved. No part of this publication may be reproduced, stored in a retrieval system, or transmitted, in any form or by any means, electronic, mechanical, photocopying, recording, or otherwise, without the prior written permission of the publisher.
Printed in the United States of America. Published simultaneously in Canada.
Library of Congress Catalog Card No. 75-3665

ISBN 0-8465-1938-0
ABCDEFGHIJKL−AL−798765

Cummings Publishing Company, Inc.
2727 Sand Hill Road
Menlo Park, California 94025

In Memorium

J. Bruce Palmer

Preface

This book provides a review of major topics on what is currently known of the prehistory of the Pacific Islands and Australia. The course of cultural development in prehistoric Oceania is traced from its beginnings on mainland Southeast Asia, thousands of years ago during the Pleistocene (Ice Age), eastward through Island Southeast Asia to Australia which was occupied over 30,000 years ago, and to New Guinea which was settled by at least 26,000 years ago.

This is followed by a discussion of the complex nature of the occupation of Island Melanesia (perhaps as early as 10,000 years ago), and Polynesia and Micronesia, both areas which appear to have been occupied within the past 4000 years.

Dealing with an area of 3,000,000 square miles, containing some 25,000 islands, it would be expected that a very irregular and complex pattern of settlement occurred. This is indeed the case, and it is a tribute to mankind's courage and ingenuity that all the islands in the Pacific were visited by man in prehistoric times. Many of these islands were settled permanently, some more than once by migrating groups in their ocean-going canoes.

Oceanic Prehistory will be of interest to the professional anthropologist and to students enrolled in courses on Oceanic cultures, Oceanic prehistory, and general prehistory. It will also be helpful to the increasing number of tourists who visit the Pacific Islands and Australia, and to the laymen who have a specific interest in Oceania or a general interest in world prehistory.

RICHARD SHUTLER, JR.

MARY ELIZABETH SHUTLER

Acknowledgments

Many of our colleagues and students have kindly provided us with information about their work. We would particularly like to thank Shirley Ahlgren, William H. Alkire, Kenneth P. Emory, Mac Marshall, Yosihiko H. Sinoto, and John P. Tandarich, who have read and made valuable comments and suggestions on the manuscript. We wish to thank John Tandarich and William Stanley for finalizing the maps and John Hotopp for his photographic work. The National Science Foundation, the Wenner-Gren Foundation for Anthropological Research, and the Bernice P. Bishop Museum have supported financially various aspects of our own fieldwork. The staff of the Bishop Museum has aided us unstintingly in every aspect of our work in the Pacific during the past 20 years. We are also indebted to many members of the British and French Governments for their unending support of many kinds in the New Hebrides. Without their support, this paper would never have been written. The interpretations and, inevitably, any errors are our own.

About the Authors

Richard Shutler, Jr. and Mary Elizabeth Shutler have conducted ethnological and archaeological fieldwork in the Southwest Pacific since 1952 and are authors of numerous articles on their interests in Oceania.

Richard Shutler, Jr. received his B.A. and M.A. from the University of California, Berkeley and his Ph.D. from the University of Arizona. He has taught at the University of Hawaii, San Diego State University, and the University of Victoria, British Columbia. He is currently Professor and Chairman of the Department of Anthropology, University of Iowa.

Mary Elizabeth Shutler received her B.A. from the University of California, Berkeley, and her M.A. and Ph.D. from the University of Arizona. She has taught at the University of Nevada, the University of California, Davis, Sacramento State University, and the University of Hawaii. She is currently Professor of Anthropology and past chairman of the Department of Anthropology, San Diego State University.

Contents

Introduction

The story of Oceanic prehistory begins in Southeast Asia. Here the populations whose descendants
were later to settle the rest of Oceania first
evolved; here Oceanic culture first began to take
shape. The period of research into Oceanic prehistory is short. Most of the significant investigations have been undertaken since the end of
World War II, and consequently much of this work
is incomplete and unpublished. For this reason a
description of the course of cultural development
in prehistoric Oceania is difficult to attempt.
Much important data has been discovered, however,
and the broad outline of the peopling of the Pacific and the evolution of its cultures is beginning to become apparent.

In the huge area of Oceania, geographers and
anthropologists have designated a number of natural and cultural areas. There are mainland and
island Southeast Asia (see Map 2, page 9). Australia and the great Pacific Basin are others,
each with its own variety of topography, climate,
and unique flora and fauna.

1

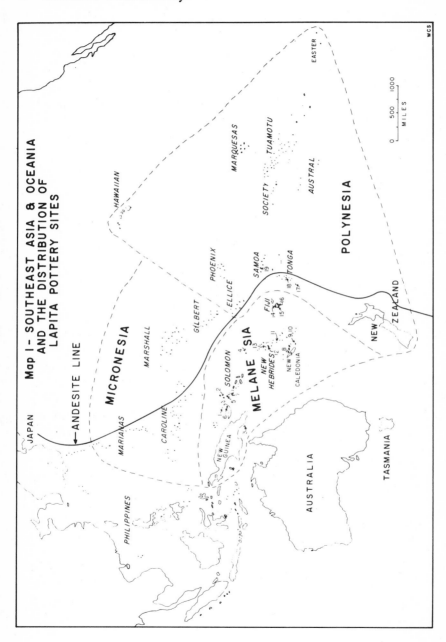

Map I - SOUTHEAST ASIA & OCEANIA AND THE DISTRIBUTION OF LAPITA POTTERY SITES

MAP 1.   Southeast Asia and Oceania: the Distribution of Lapita Pottery Sites

1. Watom Island   9. Vao, Ile des Pins
2. Ambitle Island   10. Vatcha, Ile des Pins
3. Yule Island,   11. Erueti, New Hebrides
       Hall Sound   12. Avuntari,
4. Gawa Island   New Hebrides
5. Sohano, Buka Island   13. Aore, New Hebrides
6. Talasea Area,   14. Natunuku, Fiji
       New Britain   15. Yanuca, Fiji
7. North Coast,   16. Sigatoka
       Bougainville   17. To 2, Tonga
8. Site 13, New   18. Tunuga, Tonga
       Caledonia   19. Upolu, Samoa

     Outside of Southeast Asia and Australia, the
Pacific islands traditionally have been divided
into three subareas (see Map 1). In the west,
close to Asia and Australia, is Melanesia (the
"black islands") composed of continental islands,
including New Guinea, with a scattering of volcanic islands and coral atolls. Polynesia (the
"many islands") is flung far to the east. With
Easter Island close to the coast of South America,
the Hawaiian Islands far to the north, and New
Zealand lying out of the tropics to the south, the
great Polynesian triangle embraces many island
types with volcanic islands being the most predom-
inant. To the north Micronesia (the "small islands") consists mainly of coral atolls. In the
west, Micronesia is close to Asia and shares cultural traits with Asia, while in the east it is
closer to Polynesia and Melanesia, sharing cultural similarities with these areas. The differences
between Melanesia, Polynesia, and Micronesia have

been exaggerated in the past.   There are no sharp boundaries separating them, and they have many cultural similarities.   Nevertheless, differences of topography, climate, and resources allow us to distinguish generally between the cultures of the three areas.   The areas to be considered then, in this module, are: Southeast Asia and Australia, Melanesia, Polynesia, and Micronesia.

During the Pleistocene, Southeast Asia was little affected climatically by the great ice sheets of the Northern Hemisphere, although some regions may have been a bit cooler than they are today.   Parts of Australia also may have been cooler and more moist.   The major result of the glacial maxima was to expose great areas of land, as sea levels dropped when so much of the world's moisture was caught up in glaciers and ice sheets in the Northern Hemisphere.   During times of glacial maxima the great Sunda Shelf connected many of the islands of Southeast Asia to the mainland, while the Sahul Shelf connected Australia and New Guinea (see Maps 2 and 3, pp. 9 and 32).   It should be noted, however, that in spite of this previous land connection, the Australian and New Guinea (Papuan) biotas are in many ways distinct. This is not because of the physiographic barrier of Torres Strait, but because of the basically different climates and vegetations of the two areas (Keast, 1973).   The islands of the south and central Pacific do not seem to have been particularly affected by glacial advances and retreats, and in any event, there is no indication of human occupation of most of these islands before the advent of postglacial times.

Distances are vast in the Pacific (Map 1), but land masses are small and enormously varied in size and environment.   Southeast Asia, Australia, and the great islands of New Guinea and New Zealand contain many different environments: high snowcapped mountains, low coastal plains, river valleys, bush jungles, and barren deserts. The smaller continental islands are also diverse. Lying close to Asia and Australia they exhibit a diversity of soil types, sedimentary rocks, and a rich flora and fauna.

Volcanic islands abound, raised sometimes to great heights above sea level, and often have wet sides where clouds blown by prevailing winds drop their moisture and dry sides where precipitation is light. The floral assemblages of these high islands change as one goes from their wet to their dry sides and also as one ascends from the low coastal plains to the crests of the interior mountains. Some high islands are ancient and eroded with deep and fertile soils, while others have arisen only recently from the ocean depths and are little eroded with a thin soil cover. Many of these islands have areas freshly covered with lava flows offering few resources for a human population.

Coral atolls are found everywhere in Oceania but are especially abundant in Micronesia. Built up by coral polyps on the surfaces of submarine volcanic mountains, some of these islands have been raised well above sea level by tectonic movements; others lie only just above high tide, while some appear above the surface only at low tide. Atolls tend to be extremely small in land area, often with a central lagoon that developed as the coral slowly accumulated around the perimeter of a volcanic peak. The coral continued to rise to find optimum conditions of depth, warmth, and salinity as the central volcanic peak slowly sank. Atolls are rich in marine life and are havens for

sea birds. Some atolls are dry, especially in the doldrums belt along the equator, attracting little precipitation because of their low altitude.
Since atolls have thin soil and are subject to salt spray from the sea, their flora is limited.
Many plants imported by man must be cunningly and carefully nurtured to maturity.

Island Southeast Asia, which was connected to the mainland at times during the Pleistocene, supports a great diversity of plant and animal life and can easily support hunting and gathering populations (see Map 2, p. 9). New Guinea and its surrounding islands and the continent of Australia have never been connected with the Asian mainland and have developed a quite different set of plants and animals. As one moves eastward through the Pacific, the number of plant and animal genera becomes progressively fewer. Only those plants survive that could be borne on salty ocean currents, could be carried in the stomachs of birds to the islands and still germinate, or had been brought there by people. Animal life is equally limited.
Insects borne by wind currents, birds and bats that fly, small reptiles, and other creatures that may be carried by floating masses of vegetation comprise much of the fauna on Pacific Islands.
Other animals were brought by man: dogs, pigs, chickens, and rats (the last presumably by accident).

Though the number of genera is fewer, the isolation of the true Oceanic islands has resulted in a proliferation of endemic species within these fewer genera through genetic drift. While an Asian jungle is composed of an enormous variety of plant and animal types, the jungle of a Pacific island, which is equally dense and lush, is composed of only a few plant and animal types.

        The continental masses of Asia and Australia
and the plethora of Pacific Islands are all separated from one another, many by hundreds of miles
of ocean.   There are some 25,000 islands in the
3,000,000 square miles of the Pacific Ocean, and
ocean currents flow back and forth.   The winds
shift their directions seasonally, so that it is
possible to sail in almost any direction if one
waits for the right season and the right current.
Thus, the ocean's vastness, which in so many parts
of the world has formed a barrier to culture contact, has offered a means of movement in the Pacific.   Coastal areas of widely separated islands
often have been closely linked in culture and language because of the ease of travel by water.
Mountain areas of the large islands of Melanesia
are often sharply separated from coastal areas of
the same island, having widely disparate traditions, simply because travel from the coast to the
interior is fraught with innumerable difficulties.
        Differences of topography, climate, water and
soil, plant and animal resources, and ease of contact with other people all have called forth from
the human inhabitants of Oceania a variety of cultural responses to natural milieus.   Typhoons
(hurricanes) sweep the Pacific, washing away soils
and destroying agricultural crops.   These storms
frequently bring famine in their wake, forcing
people to migrate.   Much of Oceania lies along the
Pacific circle, an area of intense volcanic and
tectonic activity, and even today islands appear
and vanish.   The alternation of plenty and famine,
the changing possibilities of isolation and contact, and movements necessitated by volcanic eruptions have produced cultures that throughout their
history have demonstrated a continuing ability to
adjust and readjust to changing conditions.

Southeast Asia

The story of the human occupation of Oceania begins on the Continent and in the islands of Southeast Asia. Man has long occupied this part of the
world. Remains of a hominid, Meganthropus paleo-
javanicus, similar to the African Australopithecines, were found in the Lower Pleistocene Djetis
beds at Sangiran, Java (Map 2; Jacob, 1972).
    The well-known Pithecanthropus finds dis-
covered by Dubois in Java at the end of the 19th
century have been assigned, together with similar
forms from Europe, Africa, western Asia, and China
to the genus and species Homo erectus. This species of man is characterized by a thick-walled,
low-vaulted skull, a large palate and teeth, and
a face with massive browridges and marked prognathism. In the size of the brain and other charac-
teristics, Homo erectus is considered transitional
between the Australopithecines and Homo sapiens.
The Modjokerto child (a Homo erectus of Pithecanthropus type found in the Djetis beds at Modjokerto) dates 1.9 ± 0.4 million years (Jacob, 1972).

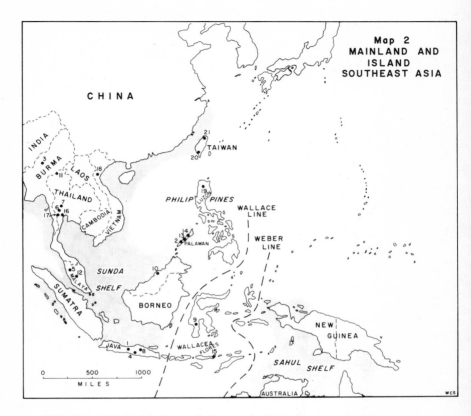

MAP 2.   Mainland and Island Southeast Asia

1. Sangiran, Java
2. Tabon Cave, Palawan
3. Anyathian Sites,
       Burma
4. Patjitan Area, Java
5. Kota Tampan,
       Malaysia
6. Kwae Noi River
       Sites, Thailand
7. Kwae Yoi River
       Sites, Thailand

8. Wadjak, Java
9. Tjabenge Industry,
       Celebes
10. Niah Cave, Sarawak
11. Spirit Cave,
       Thailand
12. Gua Kechil, Malaysia
13. Guri Cave, Palawan
14. Duyong Cave, Palawan
15. Liang Toge, Flores

(continued on p. 10)

16. Non Nok Tha,   19. Cagayan Valley,
      Thailand   Luzon
17. Ban Kao, Thailand   20. Fengpitou, Taiwan
18. Mount Dho, North   21. Tapenkeng, Taiwan
      Vietnam

Meganthropus lay stratigraphically below this. A
new Homo erectus find, Sragen Man, from the Kabuh
formation of Java and dating 830,000 B.P., was
discovered in 1972 (Jacob, personal communication).
During the late Pleistocene Homo erectus populations evolved into Homo sapiens. In Southeast
Asia these are represented by Homo sapiens soloensis and Homo sapiens wadjakensis from Java and by
the sapiens individuals discovered at Niah Cave
in Borneo, and at Tabon in the Philippines (Map 2).
Homo sapiens soloensis has been identified by some
as Homo erectus (Jacob, 1967).
      During the Pleistocene, Southeast Asia expe-
rienced changes in climate and topography oc-
casioned by the advances and retreats of glaciers
in the Northern Hemisphere. The Pleistocene climatic changes of Southeast Asia, though poorly
known, do not seem to have been as great as those
that took place in other parts of the world. Then,
as now, the climate was generally hot and humid
with times of increased coolness and aridity perhaps restricted to certain localities. More dra-
matic and of more consequence for the spread of
man in Oceania were the Pleistocene fluctuations
in sea level. During times of glacial maxima,
ocean levels were appreciably lower. As mentioned
earlier, much of insular Southeast Asia, including
Sumatra, Java, Borneo, and Palawan, became part of
the continent known as the Sunda Shelf (Map 2).
The Sahul Shelf similarly provided a land mass

connecting New Guinea and Tasmania to Australia
(Map 3, p. 32). During the Pleistocene, times of
low sea level favored human migration to the islands of Southeast Asia and to New Guinea and Australia, while times of high sea level provided
isolation for the divergence of gene pools and
of cultural adaptations.

LOWER PALEOLITHIC CULTURES
(Lower and Middle Pleistocene)

The Lower Paleolithic is defined as representing
the period of time from the advent of cultural
development until the last interglacial approximately 100,000 years ago. In Europe, Africa, and
western and northern Asia a subsequent Middle and
Upper Paleolithic are easily distinguishable. In
Southeast Asia the Lower Paleolithic is readily
discernible, but the Middle and Upper Paleolithic
stages are not apparent. This fact is due both to
an apparently autonomous and distinct cultural development in Southeast Asia, which makes typological equating of artifacts with those from other
areas difficult, and to the scarcity of excavated
sites. Some researchers have preferred to retain
schemes of cultural development derived from European materials and to fit Southeast Asian materials into these schemes (sometimes with considerable pushing and pulling!). Other investigators
have pointed out that the materials must be described in their own terms but have constructed
new schemes and attempted with little evidence to
encompass vast distances and periods of time. We
shall try to avoid either extreme and will simply
describe instead the materials from Southeast Asia
up to the end of the Pleistocene (see Table 1, p. 12).

TABLE 1. Southeast Asian Pleistocene Geology and
Archaeological Site Correlations

Stage	Sites	Fossil Man	Chromometric Date
Holocene	Liange Toge		3,550 B.P.*
	Ban Kao		4,000 B.P.
	Fengpitou		4,500 B.P.
	Tapenkeng		4,500 B.P.
	Gua Kechil		4,800 B.P.
	Loang Spean		6,240 B.P.
	Duyong Cave		7,000 B.P.
	Non Nok Tha		7,000 B.P.
Upper Pleistocene (Late)	Spirit Cave		11,690 B.P.
	Tabon Cave	Homo sapiens	30,000 B.P.
	Niah Cave	Homo sapiens	41,600 B.P.
	Tjabenge		?
	Wadjak	Homo sapiens wadjakensis	?
	Solo	Homo sapiens soloensis	?
Middle Pleistocene	Cagayan Valley		?
	Early Anyathian		?
	Patjitan		?
	Mount Kho		?
	Sangiran		?
	Kota Tampan		?
	Kwae Noi		?
	Kwae Yoi		?
	Kabuh	Sragen Man	830,000 B.P.
Lower Pleistocene	Cambodia		
	Modjokerto	Homo erectus (Modjokerto child)	1.9 ± 0.4 million yrs. B.P.
	Sangiran	Meganthropus paleojavanicus	

*B.P. = Before Present

The Paleolithic cultures of Southeast Asia
are not well known. The sites are few in number,
frequently of redeposited material, and in most
cases only vaguely dated. Movius' (1949) classic
description of the earliest stone tools of Southeast Asia has remained the standard description
despite more recent work. The Lower Paleolithic
cultures of Southeast Asia are characterized by
stone tools of Chopper-Chopping Tool Tradition,
which are of simple design, and by a rarity though
not a complete absence of handaxes (see Fig. 1 on
next page). A number of sites are known from both
mainland and insular environments.

Burma. The Anyathian sites of the central Irra-
waddy valley in Burma (Map 2) have yielded a two-
phase sequence of stone tools (Movius, 1949). The
early Anyathian, Middle Pleistocene in age, is in
turn divided into three subphases dating respec-
tively from a pluvial (wet period), interpluvial
(arid dry interval), and another pluvial (wet period). Tools are made of both silicified wood and
silicified tuff. The silicified wood does not
flake well and tends to cleave along lines parallel to the wood fibers, resulting in tools exhibiting flaking along only one plane and having a
squared outline. The bulk of the silicified wood
artifacts are hand-adzes, defined by Movius (1949)
as rectangular bevel-edged tools, unifacially
flaked, usually from cores (Fig. 1). The silicified tuff is mostly a fine-grained homogeneous
material that fractures conchoidally. There was a
greater variety of tools made of this material.
Choppers (unifacially flaked tools with a round or
straight cutting edge along the side or end, made
from either cores or flakes) are the largest tool
grouping (Fig. 1). Chopping tools (core tools,

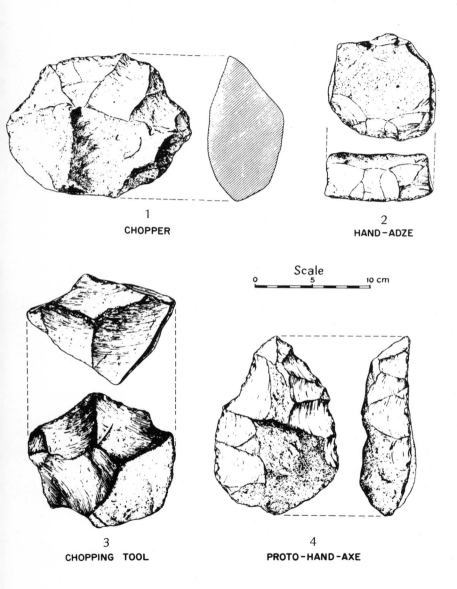

1
CHOPPER

2
HAND-ADZE

Scale
0   5   10 cm

3
CHOPPING TOOL

4
PROTO-HAND-AXE

Fig. 1. Southeast Asian Paleolithic tools. (1) chopper; (2) hand-adze; (3) chopping tool; (4) proto-hand-axe (after Movius, 1949; and with permission of the American Philosophical Society).

bifacially flaked, usually in an alternate flaking technique) and hand-adzes are also represented (Fig. 1). Tools made of this material are made on flakes as well as cores. The three subphases of the Early Anyathian can be separated stratigraphically but are almost indistinguishable on the basis of tool typology. The Late Anyathian, belonging to Late Pleistocene times, has essentially the same silicified tuff and wood tool types but with additional flakes and blades. Here the flakes seem to have been prepared before having been struck from cores. The Late Anyathian, however, lacks Levallois flakes, characteristic of archaeological assemblages in Europe, Africa, and the Middle East.

Java. The Patjitan area of the southern coast of Java (Map 2) has yielded stone industries of Middle Pleistocene age (Movius, 1949; von Koenigswald, 1936). A greater variety of tool types is found at this site, choppers being the most common. Hand-adzes similar to the Anyathian are also represented, but unlike the Anyathian, the Patjitan area has true hand-axes. A greater proportion of flake and blade tools characterizes the Patjitan area, some produced by the Levallois technique. Similar tools have been collected from a number of surface sites on Java, Sumatra, Bali, and Borneo (Soejono, 1971). Also from Java, Sangiran flakes, pre-Patjitan in age, come from the Trinil level at

Sangiran.   These flakes are Middle Pleistocene in age (Jacob, personal communication, 1973).

Malaya.   The Kota Tampan site in northwestern Malaya (Map 2) has tools made from river-rounded pebbles and on unfaceted flakes. Though Sieveking (1960), the excavator, has modified Movius' tool typology, it appears that the same types of tools found in Burma and Indonesia are represented in the Malayan collection (Fig. 1). Choppers and scrapers (simply smaller versions of choppers), chopping tools, hand-adzes (made from flakes), and some rough hand-axes were found. The site dates from late in the Second Glacial or Second Interglacial.

Thailand.   Three expeditions have collected Lower Paleolithic tools from the surfaces of sites in Thailand. Sarasin (1933a, 1933b) found a handaxe and a chopping tool that appear typologically to be Lower Paleolithic. Heider (1960) found some 104 unifacially flaked pebble tools (some can be described as choppers and some as hand-adzes) and four flake tools in the area of the Kwae Noi River (Map 2). The joint Thai-Danish expedition located two sites (Nielson, 1971), one on the Kwae Noi River. The other site, on the Kwae Yoi River (Map 2), produced a hand-axe and a chopper.

North Vietnam.   The surface collections made by Boriskovski (1969) on the slopes of Mount Kho in North Vietnam (Map 2) contain choppers, chopping tools, and two hand-axes. There is also a large number of flake tools. Four percent of them are Levallois flakes, although no Levallois or Mousterian cores were found. Throughout South Vietnam and Cambodia, pebble tools described as Acheulean

(Saurin, 1971) have been found in deposits dating
from the Second Glacial Period.

Surface finds of choppers, chopping tools,
and flakes made on Luzon and Mindanao have been
considered by some investigators to be Lower
Paleolithic (Beyer, 1948; von Koenigswald, 1960).
In recent years chopper-chopping tools have been
found in deposits of the Cagayan Valley on Luzon
(Map 2), presumably Lower Paleolithic in age
(Fox, Peralta, Paniza, Cabanilla, Ewert, Aoyagi,
Lopez, and Flores, 1971).

There can be no doubt that Lower Paleolithic
remains exist in Southeast Asia. Undoubtedly
these stone tools were made by Homo erectus, the
only contemporary man known. The paucity of the
sites and the nature of those examined make it
extremely difficult to describe Southeast Asian
Lower Paleolithic culture. Numerous investigators
have commented on the crudeness and simplicity of
the stone industries as compared to those of Europe and Africa. The rarity of handaxes and flake
tools made from prepared cores and the persistence
of pebble tools have prompted descriptions of
these cultures (based on stone tool technology) as
"backward." It is also possible that the apparent
"backwardness" may be a result of insufficient
sampling. The lack of primary activity sites like
Kalombo in Tanganyika, Torralba in Spain, or Terre
Amata in France makes it impossible to describe
Southeast Asian Lower Paleolithic culture ade-
quately.

UPPER PALEOLITHIC CULTURES
(Late or Upper Pleistocene)

The Late Anyathian described above is included by
Bordes (1968, p. 135) in the Middle Paleolithic

because of its late date and high percentage of
flake tools. Besides the increasing number of
flake tools there is little typological change in
the Anyathian sequence.

Java. Indonesia has a number of Late Pleistocene
sites. One of the earliest reported is the Solo
site on Java (Map 2). Here remains of Homo sapiens were found associated with a number of bone,
deer antler, and flake implements on river terraces.
        The Wadjak site, also on Java, has yielded
two crania of Homo sapiens. These have been compared to modern Australian aborigines. The site
is thought to be Late Pleistocene or Early Holocene in age.
        Flake tools were also discovered at a number
of different places in the Sangiran area of central Java (Map 2). A variety of tool types were
found made on short, thick flakes (von Koenigswald, 1936) in Upper Pleistocene deposits.

Celebes. Similar flake tools, usually with plain
striking platforms, obtuse flaking angles, and
clearly defined bulbs of percussion, were ob-
served on Late Pleistocene river terraces in the
Celebes. Sidescrapers, points, some crude blades,
and a pick were also found. This Tjabenge industry (Map 2) closely resembles the Sangiran industry of Java (de Terra, 1943).

Borneo. At Niah Cave in Borneo (Map 2) Late
Pleistocene deposits are well represented. Harrisson (1957) describes three main types of stone
tools for the period between 40,000 to 20,000 B.C.
(see Fig. 2a, p. 20): chopper tools (unifacially
flaked from whole pebbles), large flakes resembling the Soan of India, and small flakes. Both
choppers and large flakes tend to occur below the

small flakes that appear to be concentrated in a
band dated between 30,000 and 20,000 B.C. There
is no clear stratigraphic separation between the
different tool types, and the situation is similar
to that seen elsewhere in Southeast Asia: a remarkable persistence of Lower Paleolithic tool
types into Late Pleistocene times. At Niah, a
Homo sapiens skull was found ten inches below a
radiocarbon sample assaying at 39,600 B.C. ± 1000
years. Just below this skull was a single flake
of "Mid-Sohan" type.

Palawan. Tabon Cave in Palawan in the Philippines
(Map 2) has evidence of a long occupation beginning at a date estimated at 45,000-50,000 B.P.,
and ending at 9500 B.P. Fox (1970) distinguished
five occupation levels containing both flake and
core tools, bone remains, and scattered charcoal.
Flake Tool Industry III with a radiocarbon date of
23,200 ± 1000 B.P. was associated with remains of
Homo sapiens. The stone tools throughout the occupation levels represent a single, long-lasting,
simple flake tool tradition (see Fig. 2b, p. 22).
     From what little evidence is available it
would appear that the Upper Paleolithic stone tool
industries of Southeast Asia are predominantly
small flake tools exhibiting various shapes. Earlier forms continue to be used and there is no
sharp typological difference between industries
dating from the Middle and Late Pleistocene.
There is some evidence of the increasing use of
bone and antler as artifact material.

Taiwan. Paleolithic bamboo implements have been
reported from Taitung in eastern Taiwan, but no
description or dating of these artifacts has ap-
peared. No human bones or other artifacts have
been reported from the Late Pleistocene of Taiwan.

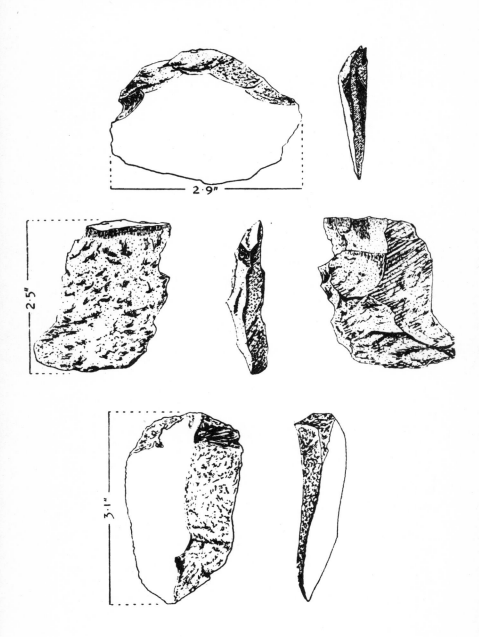

Fig. 2a.   Niah Cave flake tools (after Harrisson, 1959).

        The terminal Pleistocene of Southeast Asia marks the beginning of a new exploitative pattern, the Hoabinhian. This assemblage is distinguished by simple flake tools reminiscent of those of the Lower Paleolithic. The basic Hoabinhian implement is a waterworn pebble (see Fig. 3a, p. 23), flaked bifacially to form a continuous cutting or scraping edge around the tool. Sometimes these tools are flaked unifacially leaving the pebble cortex on one face, as seen in the Sumatralith (see Fig. 3b, p. 23). There are many used flakes, grinding and pounding tools, also made on pebbles. These implements are frequently stained with hematite. In the upper levels of Hoabinhian sites, edge-grinding of pebble tools (Fig. 3a) and/or cord-marked pottery are found. Burials from Hoabinhian sites have been described as similar in physical type to those found in Melanesia.
        Upland Hoabinhian sites have been reported in Burma, Vietnam, Thailand, Cambodia, and Malaya. These sites are described as camping places and rockshelters located near streams in forest-covered areas of eroded limestone. In Vietnam, the Malay Peninsula, and Sumatra, Hoabinhian tools have also been found in coastal shell middens. Although there is evidence of a heavy reliance on marine resources from these lowland sites, inland flora and fauna were not ignored (Gorman, 1971). The location of the sites and the variety of their floral and faunal remains appears to indicate a widespread adaptation to the ecology of Southeast Asia.

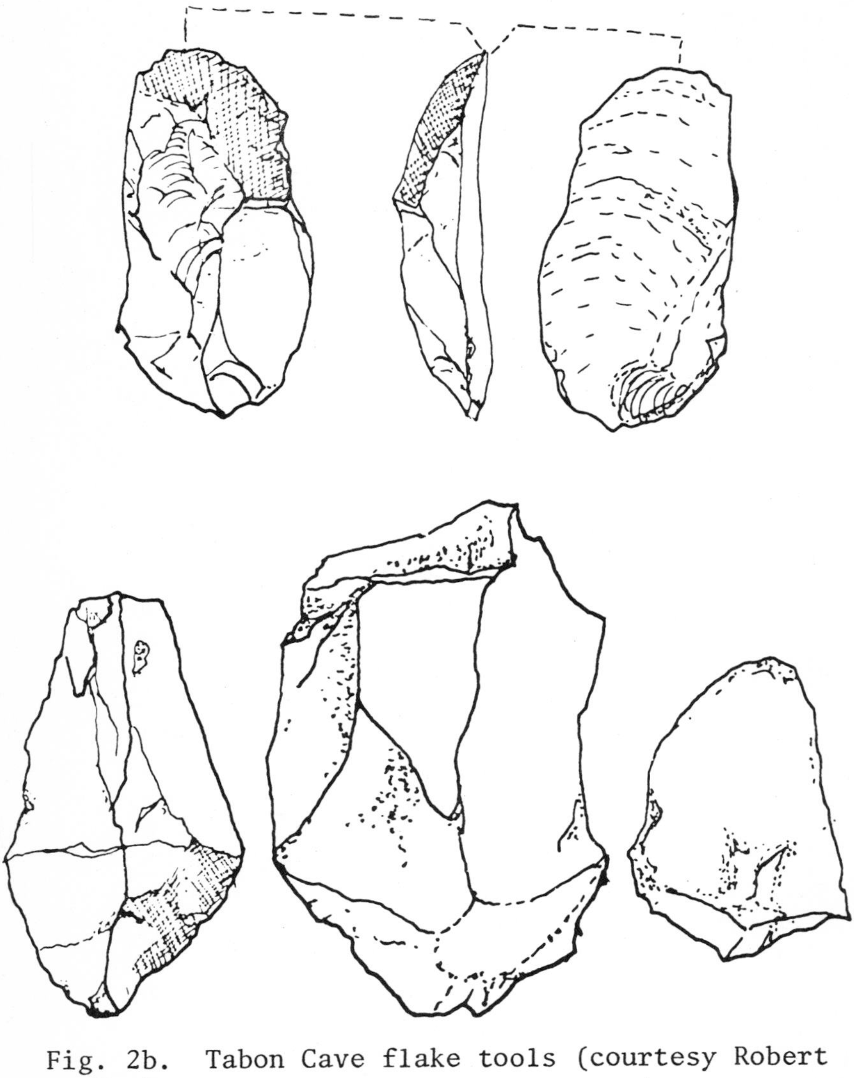

Fig. 2b.   Tabon Cave flake tools (courtesy Robert
B. Fox).

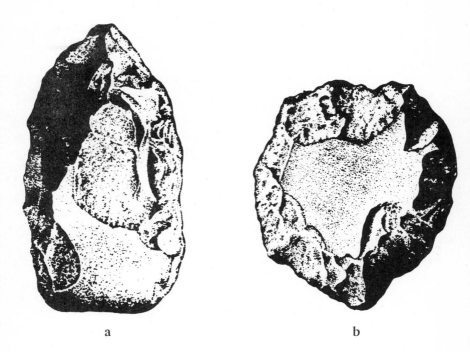

a   b

Fig. 3.   Hoabinhian tools.   (a) bifacial, edge-
ground axe; (b) unifacial Sumatralith (after
Beyer, 1952).

Dunn (1970) has suggested that the distribution of Hoabinhian sites was influenced by the
rising sea level of the Pleistocene.   By 11,000
to 10,000 B.P. insular Southeast Asia had been
cut off by sea from the mainland and the spread-
ing Hoabinhian pattern, resulting in genetic and
cultural isolation.   An exception to this may
have been the Hoabinhian sites discovered on
Sumatra, which are along the coast within sight
of the Malay Peninsula.

Radiocarbon dates from several sites, including the sequence from Spirit Cave in Thailand (Map 2), clearly indicate the long duration of the Hoabinhian. The earliest date at Spirit Cave is 11,690 ± 560 B.P., but this does not date the lower levels. Gorman (1971, p. 301) suggests a date of 13,000-14,000 B.P. for the first occupation of the site. Dates on terminal Hoabinhian come from three sites: Gua Kechil in Malaya (Map 2) at 4800 ± 800 B.P.; 7622 ± 300 B.P. at Spirit Cave in Thailand; and from Laang Spean in Cambodia, 6240 ± 70 B.P.

Floral remains have been carefully analyzed only from Spirit Cave. Here from 10,000-6,000 B.C., there is indicated that a number of plants were used, among them almonds, beans and peas, water chestnuts, peppers, cucumber, bottle gourd, and candlenut. All of these remain culturally important in Southeast Asia (Gorman, 1971, pp. 310-311). Whether or not any of these plants were actually cultivated, Gorman has pointed out that the "broad spectrum" exploitation pattern was an important preadaptation leading in the Near East to plant and animal domestication. Carl Sauer (1952) long ago pointed out that Southeast Asia may have been a very early center of food production.

In the island environments of Southeast Asia, evidence of material resembling the Hoabinhian has been found only on Sumatra so far. It is possible that the small flake tool industries of the Late Pleistocene lingered on until the spread of food production and village life. On Palawan, Fox (1967) found flake and blade tool industries at Guri Cave and Duyong Cave (Map 2). A radiocarbon date of 7000 ± 250 B.P. was obtained on the material from Duyong Cave (Fox, 1967, pp. 109-113). At Niah Cave on Borneo, Harrisson (1959) reports

that between clearly Paleolithic material and
later Neolithic polished stone tools he found in-
termediate material composed of small carefully
reworked flakes, edge-ground axes and adzes made
of pebbles. A series of skeletons from these layers has been described as "Melanoid" in character.
At Niah, ground stone axe-adzes are found dated at
10,000 years ago. From Indonesia "Mesolithic" remains are reported from numerous places (Van Heek-
eran, 1957; Jacob, 1967). The material generally
is composed of a variety of tools made from small
flakes and blades; some sites have a considerable
number of bone tools as well. Some of these tools
seem to come from quite recent levels. The material from Liang Toge in the Flores (Map 2) has a
radiocarbon date of 3550 ± 525 B.P. Numerous
burials found with these tools are described as
having both Austro-melanesian and Mongoloid char-
acteristics (Jacob, 1967).

Beginning of Food Production

The Hoabinhian pattern seems to have been followed by settled village farming. Important sites
include Non Nok Tha (Map 2) in Thailand, where
three cultural levels were distinguished. The
earliest period has incised and impressed, as well
as cord-marked pottery, grains of rice (whether
wild or domestic is not known), and bones of domestic dog, pig, and zebu cattle. From near the
top of this level came a copper-socketed tool.
The site was intermittently occupied, probably by
people practicing swidden farming with some hunting. The lowest level may date as early as the
fifth millenium B.C. and ends about 3000 B.C. In
the middle period, which dates from 3000 B.C. to
about A.D. 300, bronze was used and locally manu-
factured. The last period begins at A.D. 1100,
the time of the introduction of Buddhism and the
beginning of wet rice agriculture, marked by the
appearance of water buffalo bones (Solheim, 1972).
Ban Kao, a farming village also in Thailand (Map
2), was first occupied about 2000 B.C. Domestic
pigs were present, and as at Non Nok Tha, farming
was supplemented by hunting and gathering.

On Taiwan, Chang (1969) excavated two sites
where cord-marked pottery (Corded Ware culture)
underlay two different later Neolithic cultures.
This culture has pebbles flaked along the edges,
pitted pebbles, hoe-like implements, polished rectangular adzes, and perforated triangular points.
The pottery is cord-marked and often bears painted
or incised decoration. An early radiocarbon date
of 19,670 ± 450 B.P. for Corded Ware culture is
suspect, but the culture may start about 9000 B.C.

Pollen profiles from central Taiwan suggest
repeated forest burning beginning at 9000 B.C.,
lasting until the beginning of intensive agriculture at 2500 B.C. Chang (1969) correlates this
burning with the forest clearing accompanying
swidden farming of root crops by Corded Ware culture people. Although this conclusion is speculative, it accords well with the Corded Ware culture's stone tool kit, which is suitable for plant
cultivation and hunting. A suggestion of early
plant cultivation in Taiwan also fits well with
the indication of early cultivation far to the
west in Thailand. In eastern Indonesia, evidence
of agriculture and pottery making began on Timor
at least 4500 years ago (Glover, 1971).

At the Fengpitou site (Map 2), the Lungshanoid culture followed the Corded Ware culture. In
the Lungshanoid culture, subsistence was based on
agriculture supplemented by shellfish gathering,
fishing, and hunting. Typical artifacts include
rectangular and rudimentary stepped adzes, semilu-
nar and rectangular stone knives, stemmed arrow-
heads, late halberds, jade and serpentine artifacts, and extensive use of bone and shell as
artifact material. There is a wide variety of
pottery types, including cord-marked and the characteristic thin black pottery of the Lungshan.

Chang (1969) suggests that the Lungshanoid culture at 2500 B.C. brought rice and millet agriculture and Austronesian language to Taiwan.

At Tapenkeng (Map 2) the Yuan-shan culture (2500 B.C.) was also agriculturally based with hunting and fishing but with no evidence of shell-fish collecting. Shouldered and stepped adzes, arrow and spear heads, spindle whorls, and typical Yuan-shan pottery were found (Chang, 1969).

The agriculture of Oceania (Melanesia, Poly-nesia, and most of Micronesia) is based on the cultivation of crops native to Southeast Asia, principally yams and taro, and on the domesticated pig and chicken, also of Southeast Asian origin. In precontact times rice was found only in the Marianas (Solenberger, 1967). Rice was present at Non Nok Tha in Thailand before 4000 B.C., although it is not known if it was cultivated. To Gorman (1971) the presence of stone knives resembling rice harvesting knives from Indonesia at Spirit Cave about 6500 B.C. suggests that rice agricul-ture may have started by this time. However, root crop agriculture must have been well established in Southeast Asia before rice was widely culti-vated. Yen (1971) points out that there is no environmental barrier to the spread of rice agri-culture to the Pacific Islands, and therefore, the barrier that prevented its transference must have been a cultural one. The suggestion of very early root crop farming fits well with the evidence of early farming on New Guinea, where radiocarbon dates earlier than 5000 B.C. on pig remains (Bul-mer, 1966), (probably associated with plant cul-tivation) clearly antedate all but the very ear-liest experimentation with cereal cultivation in Southeast Asia.

The reconstruction of Southeast Asian prehistory has been built more on speculation than on excavation. Older theories of migrations of people bearing differently shaped adzes into the area have now been abandoned. Instead, a number of local Neolithic cultures are presumed to have developed, having different forms of quadrangular adzes, various pottery traditions (some of complicated form and having elaborate painted, incised, and impressed designs), knives of several forms, bark beaters, and fishing gear. Most investigators have remarked on the similarities of many Southeast Asian Neolithic artifacts to those of the Lungshanoid cultures of China, and the beginning of the Southeast Asian Neolithic is attributed to the spread of populations of Mongoloid physical type from China. Presumably these migrations ultimately pushed some of the original inhabitants out into the Pacific. The picture is complicated further by the fact that in some areas some tool industries similar to those of the earlier Hoabinhian and Small Flake Tradition seem to linger on until very recent times.

At some point, perhaps as early as 3000 B.C., bronze technology began to diffuse throughout Southeast Asia. Bronze artifacts never completely replaced stone tools. The diffusion of iron working took place largely after the beginning of the Christian era, and metal working did not spread beyond Southeast Asia to the Pacific Islands, except to western New Guinea (de Bruijn, 1962).

Because of the priority of known dates in Southeast Asia, Solheim (1972) has proposed that the main lines of diffusion were not from China to Southeast Asia. Rather he argues that agriculture and metal working first started in Southeast Asia, and that the Chinese Neolithic phases (Yangshao and Lungshan) developed from the Hoabinhian and moved north.   Although this provocative reconstruction is highly tentative, it reminds us that the course of cultural development in Southeast Asia was by no means simple, and the means and directions of diffusion were many and varied.

Australia

Man entered the continent of Australia (see Map 3, next page) sometime during the Late Pleistocene. Low sea levels, correlated to glacial maxima, existed sometime between 40,000 to 100,000 B.P. and again at about 18,000 to 20,000 B.P. (Jennings, 1971). However, the first humans to come to Australia must have made part of the trip by watercraft. Even when sea levels were lowest, the great ocean trenches in the area of Wallacea (Map 2) prevented land connections between New Guinea and Australia and the mainland of Southeast Asia.[1] [All notes appear at the end of the book.] Two routes could have been practical for men with only simple watercraft, perhaps only floating logs or rafts. A chain of islands barely visible from one to another would have extended from Borneo through the Celebes (attached by the Sunda Shelf to the Asiatic mainland) and Moluccas to New Guinea (connected to Australia by the Sahul Shelf) (Map 2). A second route lay across the straits from Timor to Australia and, during times of low sea level, presented only a slightly longer water route than

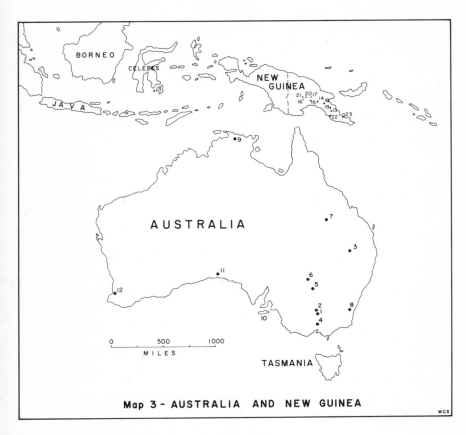

Map 3 - AUSTRALIA AND NEW GUINEA

MAP 3.   Australia and New Guinea

1. Kow Swamp,
   Australia
2. Cohuna Skull,
   Australia
3. Talgai Cranium,
   Australia
4. Keilor Cranium,
   Australia

5. Lake Mungo, Australia
6. Lake Menindee,
   Australia
7. Kenniff Cave,
   Australia
8. Burrill Rockshelter,
   Australia

9. Oenpelli Area,
   Australia
10. Kangaroo Island,
    Australia
11. Koonalda Cave,
    Australia
12. Devil's Lair,
    Australia
13. Kosipe Site,
    New Guinea
14. Kafiavana Rock-
    shelter, New
    Guinea
15. Kiowa Rockshelter,
    New Guinea
16. Yuku Rockshelter,
    New Guinea
17. Niobe Rockshelter,
    New Guinea
18. Batari Rockshelter,
    New Guinea
19. Aibura Rockshelter,
    New Guinea
20. Maton Site, New
    Guinea
21. Kuk Site, New Guinea
22. Nebira 4 Site, New
    Guinea
23. Wanigela,
    New Guinea

that between the Celebes and New Guinea. After the acquisition of suitable watercraft, landings could have been made anywhere along the northern Australian coast. Tasmania was connected to Australia by the Sahul Shelf and may have been first occupied during the latest period of low sea level.

Australian Pleistocene climate cannot be definitely described at this time. It was formerly believed that glacial advances meant increased rainfall and vegetation, which supported the Pleistocene marsupial megafauna. Recent studies have shown that glaciation was severely limited to high elevations in Tasmania and in the Snow mountains of Australia. Changes in precipitation were regionally varied, and the Australian deserts were probably arid during Pleistocene times. It is therefore possible that the extinction of the Australian Pleistocene fauna was not due to sweeping climatic change but was the result of hunting by

man and his dog, and particularly a result of the
vegetational changes induced by the widescale use
of fire in hunting (Jones, 1968).
    A number of skeletal remains of Pleistocene
man have been found in Australia. With a possible
exception of the Kow Swamp material, they are all
identifiable as Homo sapiens and similar to,
though not identical with, modern Australian aborigines. Furthermore, resemblances have been
noted between these remains and those of the Java-
nese Pleistocene men.[2] Among the Australian
skulls, the remains of over 30 individuals discovered at Kow Swamp in northern Victoria (Map 3)
are morphologically the most primitive.   Indeed,
they exhibit so many similarities to Homo erectus
that Thorne and Macumber (1972) have assigned them
to that species rather than to Homo sapiens. However, while they have certain similarities to Homo
erectus, they do not fit the morphological pattern
recently defined by Macintosh and Larnach (1972)
that occurs only in Homo erectus. In spite of the
early appearance of the Kow Swamp material, five
radiocarbon dates place the skeletal remains between 10,000 and 8000 years ago. The nearby Cohuna skull (Map 3) has been described as morphologically primitive (it appears to belong to the
Kow Swamp series), as has the Talgai skull from
Queensland (Map 3), and the Mossgiel skeleton from
New South Wales. Of these three, only Talgai is
reasonably well dated. Recent work at the Talgai
Site, near Warwik, Queensland, indicates that the
Talgai cranium is at least 14,000 years old, and
may be as much as 20,000 years old (Hendy, Rafter,
and Macintosh, 1972). The morphologically more
modern Keilor cranium from Victoria (Map 3) seems
to be accurately dated at 12,900 ± 120 B.P. (Macintosh, 1972). The similar and nearby Green Gully

finds date from about 6500 years ago (Mulvaney, 1969). The most ancient dated Australian skeletal remains are those of a young woman, partially cremated, found near Lake Mungo in western New South Wales (Map 3) and dated at 25,000 B.P. There is a radiocarbon date of 32,000 B.P. from the same site (Bowler, Jones, Allen, and Thorne, 1970). Surprisingly, though displaying a number of primitive features, these remains are the most modern in appearance with many points of resemblance to present-day aborigines (Bowler, Jones, Allen, and Thorne, 1970).

Investigators have proposed various theories to account for the variation seen in modern aborigines. Birdsell (1967), for example, postulates that the modern aborigine is the hybrid result of migrations of Negritos, Murrayians, and Carpentarians to Australia. Others (for example, Macintosh, 1963; and Abbie, 1966) feel that the aborigine represents a single stock, which has differentiated because of long isolation, small population, consequent genetic drift, and environmental adaptation. At this time fossil remains from both Australia and Southeast Asia are too few to solve the problem, and genetic (Kirk, 1971) and linguistic studies (Tryon, 1971) are not yet of much help.

Stemming from his work at Kenniff Cave (Map 3), Queensland, Mulvaney (1969) proposed that Australian prehistory could be divided into three sequential phases. The original phase beginning with the first migration is characterized by pebble, core, and flake stone tools, when many, if not all, tools were used unhafted (see Fig. 4, next page). More recently this phase has been named the Australian Core and Scraper Tradition (Bowler, Jones, Allen, and Thorne, 1970). An

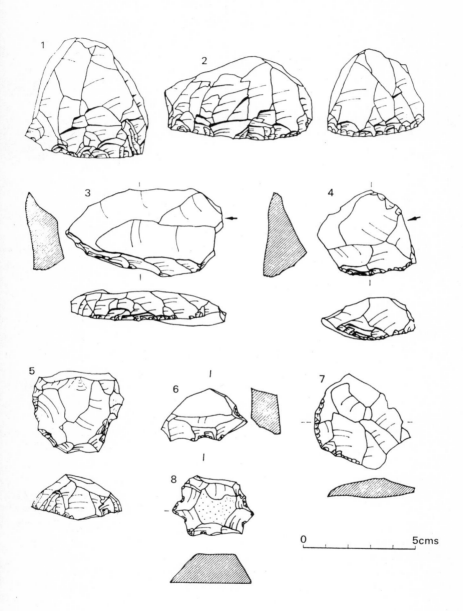

Fig. 4. Australian Core and Scraper Tradition
artifacts.   (1-2) core tools (horse hoof cores);
(3-6) steep-edged scrapers;   (7) flat scraper;
(8) concave scraper (after Bowler, et al., 1970).

Inventive Phase, marked by the spread of a Small-
Tool Tradition (Gould, 1973), began perhaps as
early as 10,000 years ago. The Small-Tool Tradition adds new forms to the Australian tool kit,
but does not replace the older core and flake
tools. During this time hafting became more common, and many new forms were invented, as Australians began the process of adjusting to their
newly won continent. The last few centuries before European contact comprise the Adaptive Phase,
during which the number and variety of stone tools
decreased in some parts of Australia. Mulvaney
(1969 and elsewhere) suggests that this decrease
was caused by an increasing use of locally available organic material for tool manufacture, indicating a closer adaptation to the environment.

Core and Scraper Tradition. Tools of this tradition (Fig. 4) have been found widely in Australia
(Mulvaney, 1969; Gould, 1973). They represent the
earliest tools known, and in many areas they have
remained in use into the present century. Typical
are large steep-edged cores, usually called horse-
hoof cores and probably used for pounding and
heavy scraping and planing activities. There are
other forms of cores and a variety of scrapers
(unifacially worked flake tools of varied design
and suited to a variety of functions). Some of
the scrapers show retouch and some do not. Also
found are simple pebble tools that bear general
resemblances to Paleolithic tools of Southeast
Asia. Tools of this sort have been found in New

South Wales at Lake Mungo, associated with human
cremations dating between 25,000 and 32,000 years
ago (Fig. 4). At Lake Menindee (Map 3), near Lake
Mungo, a radiocarbon date of 26,300 ± 1500 B.P.
(based on charcoal from Bed B, Area II) is apparently associated with two flakes and extinct mar-
supials (Jones, 1968, p. 187). Burrill Lake Rockshelter, also in New South Wales (Map 3), has
unpatterned flake and core tools, many showing
retouch, in its lowest levels, dated at about
20,000 B.P. In Queensland the important Kenniff
Cave has similar tools in its lowest levels dated
at 14,000 B.P. Four stratified rockshelters in
the Oenpelli area of Arnhem Land (Map 3) yielded
large chipped scrapers dating from 18,000 to
22,900 years ago. These scrapers were associated
with edge-ground grooved axes, an association indicating a surprising antiquity for the latter
implement in Australia, antedating the appearance
of edge-grinding in Southeast Asia. For South
Australia the Kartan Culture contains horse-hoof
cores and large flakes that may date to at least
10,000 years ago. This material was collected
from the surface of Kangaroo Island (Map 3). A
stratified rockshelter on Kangaroo Island has
yielded a radiocarbon date of 10,940 B.P., though
it is associated with stone tools and flakes not
closely resembling those collected from the surface (Lampert, 1972). Also from South Australia,
the human use of Koonalda Cave (Map 3), a flint
quarry, dates between 22,000 and 15,000 years ago.
Most of the material represents waste flakes from
quarrying activities. One of the investigators
(Wright, 1971) believes that other lithics are too
amorphous to be considered tools. The other in-
vestigator, Gallus (1971), is struck with resemblances between this collection and tools of the

European Paleolithic. The cave also has rock engravings carved into the soft limestone walls by
fingers or sharp sticks and stones. Parallel
crossing lines and meanders are also found. If,
as seems likely, the engravings date from the same
time as the deposit in the cave, then Australian
rock art must have had its beginnings in Pleistocene times.

From Devil's Lair, a small cave near Augusta
in extreme southwest Western Australia (Map 3),
Dortch and Meirilees (1973) report a flake and
core stone industry with numerous bones, some of
which they believe were hafted. They date these
hafted tools to at least 14,000 B.P., and possibly
to 25,000 B.P.

All the material excavated from Tasmania (Map
3) resembles this early Core and Scraper Tradition. Tasmania was occupied before 8000 years ago
and evidently was cut off from effective contact
with the mainland of Australia by the rising
waters in Bass Strait before the spread of the
Small Tool Tradition, the dingo, and spear-
thrower. None of these have been found in Tasmania (Jones, 1966).

Small Tool Tradition. The Inventive Phase of Australian prehistory sees the introduction and
spread of a number of small flake tools well de-
signed for certain specialized tasks. Included
in this Small Tool Tradition (see Fig. 5, next
page) are: tula adze-flakes (Fig. 5a), broad
flakes with a steep flaked edge set in a resin
handle or even on one end of a spear-thrower
(Gould, 1973; Mulvaney, 1969). Burin adze flakes
have been so resharpened on the original cutting
edge that they have been turned in the hafting and
sharpened on the opposite edge, resulting in
pointed flakes. The "elouera" is a triangular

1

2

3

4

C M

Fig. 5.   Australian small tool tradition artifacts.
(1) tula adzes; (2) eloueras; (3) fabricator; (4)
pirri points (courtesy South Australian Museum,
Adelaide).

sectioned flake with a broad blunted back (Fig.
5b). "Fabrications" are small tools flaked bifacially on opposite edges producing a square shaped
tool (Fig. 5c). Unifacially flaked points called
pirri points (Fig. 5d), bifacially flaked points,
small backed blades and flakes, some triangular or
crescentic shape, are classed as microliths.
These new tools did not replace the older forms
but were used side by side with long-popular forms
of core and scraper tools. Some bone and shell
tools also made their appearance. The Small Tool
Tradition did not appear simultaneously throughout
Australia. Small tools are present at some sites
as early as 10,000 years ago and seem to be almost
everywhere by 3000 B.C. Nor is each tool type of
the Small Tool Tradition everywhere represented.
Each tool type has its own distribution. The
Small Tool Tradition is not a single industrial
complex, but rather it varies in different parts
of Australia where different small tools were invented or borrowed to be used for specific tasks
in the exploitation of a particular environment.
     The appearance of these small tools raises
the question of cultural çontact between Australia
and Southeast Asian cultures. There certainly are
resemblances between the older Core and Scraper
Tradition of Australia and Southeast Asian Paleolithic tools. Unifacially flaked pebbles resembling Hoabinhian ones have been found in Australia,
and edge-ground axes are found in both areas,
though much earlier in Australia. In these cases,

the tools compared are so simple and so amorphous
that we feel it is impossible to decide whether
resemblances indicate cultural contact or are
simply fortuitous. In simple percussion flaking
without extensive core preparation or retouching
only a limited variety of shapes of flakes and
cores are produced, and these are likely to appear anywhere at any time stone is flaked.

The Small Tool Tradition of Australia is composed of a number of quite specific tool types,
some of which are duplicated in "microlithic"
tools of Holocene age from various places in Southeast Asia, especially Indonesia. Unfortunately,
these Southeast Asian small tools are poorly known
and the precise dates and cultural correlates of
the stone tools are unknown. Various scholars
have suggested a migration to Australia in the
early Holocene times bringing small tools, the
dingo, the spear-thrower, and perhaps even a new
race of men (Thorne, 1971). Dortch and Meirilees
(1973) suggest that the dingo was in Australia by
6500 B.C.; however, Macintosh (1974) doubts the
context of these dates and suggests that a date
for the dingo in Australia is about 3000 B.P.,
based on present reliable evidence.

Proto-Contact Period. The Australian aborigines
never adopted agriculture in spite of the fact
that at least in late prehistoric times Australians had regular contact with agricultural people.
Trepang fleets from Macassar (Celebes) visited
Arnhem Land annually (Macknight, 1972). Boats
stayed from a few days to several weeks collecting
the sea slugs, and then boiling, gutting, and dry-
ing them to be traded ultimately to China where
they were made into soup valued as a delicacy.
Contact with the aborigines during these expedi-

tions was usually peaceful. Australians served as
crewmen on the Macassarese praus. Numerous ele-
ments were incorporated into aboriginal culture:
dugout canoes with sails, metal fish hooks, van
Dyke beards, smoking pipes, bark painting motifs,
sculpture in the round, grave posts, and many
Macassarese words. Also, the coasts of Australia
were undoubtedly visited many times by Asian ships
blown off course by storms.

The people of the Cape York area of Australia
and the Torres Straits area of New Guinea (Map 3)
have been in close contact for a long time. Close
resemblance between the Cape York and New Guinea
crania (closest to Cape York) attest to this (Macintosh and Larnach, 1973). Again numerous items
have been borrowed by the Australians from their
agricultural neighbors: drum types, outrigger
canoes, house forms, hero cults, initiation cere-
monies. Many of the same plants (yam, taro, arrow-
root, and so on) were found on both sides of the
Torres Straits but were cultivated in New Guinea
and gathered wild in Australia. Extensive trading
took place between New Guinea and Australian
groups, though foodstuffs do not seem to have been
traded.

White (1971) has pointed out that the aborigines of Cape York and Arnhem Land had at their
disposal rich marine and land resources which they
were exploiting satisfactorily. They simply had
no need for the extra food that agriculture would
bring. It can be further pointed out that in
cases of cultural contact not all members of each
involved society meet, but rather, some individuals of each society with their specialized knowl-
edge of their respective society's culture meet
for specific purposes in a "contact community."
Thus, the cultural items likely to be transmitted

from one group to another are limited (Spicer,
1971). Male Macassarese trepang collectors camped
for a short time on an Australian beach are not
the most efficient or likely teachers of Asian agricultural techniques. Neither would Melanesian
traders intent on a good bargain be likely to
transmit techniques of swidden agriculture, a
process that usually takes an intent anthropologist a year of close observation to understand.
There is no evidence reported from either Arnhem
Land or Cape York of sharp population increases
triggered by either migration or internal growth
that would strain wild food resources and make
experiments with food production vital to survival
(Binford and Binford, 1968). The items transmitted were, instead, ideas and objects known to the
foreign members of the contact community and readily accepted by the Australians as novelties use-
ful to their ceremonial life, or tools and weap-
ons of obvious utility in an already well-adjusted
hunting and gathering economy.

Melanesia

Geographically, Melanesia (see Map 4, next page) includes the huge island of New Guinea and its fringing islands (the Schouten Islands off its northwestern end, the Trobriands, Woodlark, D'Entrecasteaux, and the Louisiade off the eastern end). To the northeast of New Guinea is located the Bismarck Archipelago including New Britain, New Ireland, and the Admiralty Islands. Moving southeastward in succession are located Bougainville, the Solomons, Santa Cruz, Torres, Banks, and the New Hebrides. To the southwest lie New Caledonia and the Loyalty Islands and to the east Fiji.

The Melanesian islands lie west of the Andesite line (Map 1) and in pre-Pleistocene times were connnected to the continental block. Hence, many of them are continental islands with sedimentary rocks and rich and varied soil types. Of more recent origin are volcanic and raised coral islands.

Melanesians, though extremely varied, are predominantly dark-skinned, have woolly, curly

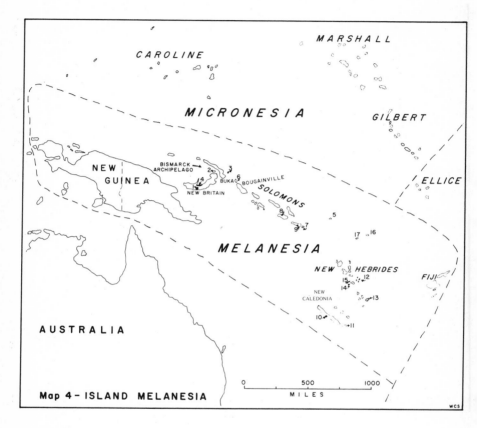

MAP 4.   Island Melanesia

1. Kandrian Area,
        New Britain
2. Watom Island
3. Ambitle Island
4. Talasea Area,
        New Britain
5. Gawa Island
6. Buka Island
7. Santa Ana Island
8. Poha Valley Site,
        Guadalcanal
9. Pauma, San Cristobal
        Island
10. Site 13,
        New Caledonia

11. Vao and Vatcha,   14. Fila Island, Efate,
     Ile des Pins   New Hebrides
12. Central New   15. Mele Island, Efate,
     Hebrides   New Hebrides
13. Futuna, New   16. Anuta Island
     Hebrides   17. Tikopia Island

hair, and are generally of short stature. They
possess some prognathism, a varying thickness of
the lips, and a considerable breadth of the nasal
tip. They vary in beard and body hair. Pygmy groups
are found in the interior of New Guinea, apparently representing an in situ divergence from surrounding people (Semple, Simmons, and Graydon,
1956). Present evidence from blood groupings
(Simmons, 1956; Swindler, 1955) and anthropometric
studies (Swindler, 1962) indicate no genetic relationship between the dark-skinned people of the
Pacific and those of Africa. Present-day Melanesians must bear some relationship to the early
Holocene inhabitants of Southeast Asia described
as Austromelanesian or Melanoid.
     There are two main language groups within
Melanesia: the Austronesian and the Papuan. The
distribution of Papuan languages is confined to
New Guinea, mainly in the interior, to parts of
eastern Indonesia, to parts of the New Britain
archipelago and Solomon Islands, and to parts of
the Duff and Santa Cruz islands. Most of the
Papuan languages of New Guinea have been grouped
into a single macrophylum of distantly related
languages. It has been assumed by most linguists
that the great diversity of the Papuan languages
indicates a great antiquity.
     Austronesian languages, which probably orig-
inated in Southeast Asia, are found scattered from

Madagascar through parts of mainland and most of
Island Southeast Asia, along the coast of New
Guinea, through most of Island Melanesia, and in
all of Micronesia and Polynesia.   Dyen (1971) has
suggested that the New Guinea-Bismarck-Solomons
area with its great linguistic diversity may be
the homeland, but other considerations led him
also to propose Taiwan.   However, the linkage of
Austronesian with the Thai and Kadai languages of
Southeast Asia and Southern China by Benedict
(1942, 1966, 1967) probably puts the ultimate
homeland back on the mainland.   On the basis of
analysis of common words, we can infer that the
Austronesian settlers of Melanesia were agricul-
turalists growing root and tree crops.   They also
kept pigs, exploited available marine resources,
and were accomplished sailors.   Northern Melanesia
remains a likely homeland of the Oceanic subdivision of the Austronesian languages, a subdivision
that contains almost all the languages spoken in
Melanesia, Polynesia, and Micronesia.

NEW GUINEA

Because of its great size and variety of topography and climate, New Guinea has a diversity of
cultures and an archaeological record that distin-
guishes it from the rest of Melanesia.   The prehistory of this area will be discussed separately
from that of Island Melanesia.   New Guinea, like
Australia, yields evidence of human occupation
during the late Pleistocene.   Even though the
Pleistocene climate of New Guinea has hardly been
studied, it seems that much of the area was probably warm and humid.   During times of glacial maxima, ice seems to have covered the high mountains
of the interior at as low a point as 2500 or 3500

meters of elevation. The tree line may have been
as much as 1500 meters lower than at present.

The earliest archaeological sites known are
located in the highlands of the Territory of Papua-
New Guinea. The open site of Kosipe (Map 4) located some 135 kilometers north of Port Moresby in
the central district, has evidence of man's presence incorporated into layers of ash from volcanic
eruptions of Mount Lamington. Analysis of radiocarbon dates indicates a long period of human occupation beginning at about 25,000 B.C. Waisted
blades (bifacially flaked blades indented on opposite edges to form a waist presumably to permit
hafting) were found associated with flaked axe-
adze blades of lenticular cross-section. In the
top artifact-bearing level, dating around 7000
B.C., one ground axe-adze blade was found (White,
Crook, and Buxton, 1970).

At the Kafiavana Rockshelter in the Eastern
Highlands district (Map 4), the lowest culture-
bearing unit, lying below a radiocarbon sample
dating about 8700 B.C., contains large pebble
tools, and flakes and fragments of small ground
axe-adze blades. Fragments large enough to be
identified as symmetrically bevelled, lenticular
cross-sectioned, ground axe-adze blades were found
in a level dating to about 7500 B.C. These tool
types persisted throughout the occupation of the
site, which lasted, with a gap between about 3000
and 2000 B.C., until recent times. Although the
stone tool industry was remarkably stable during
this period, the proportion of large pebble tools
and retouched flakes decreased through time and
there was an increase in scrapers and unretouched,
used flakes. No waisted blades were found. At a
level dating to approximately 4500 B.C. pig bone
was found (White, 1967).

Kiowa Rockshelter in the Chimbu District, Eastern Highlands (Map 4) is a stratified site with a dated sequence. The earliest cultural unit, dating between 8400 and 4000 B.C., contained pebble tools and a considerable variety of flake tools. These types of tools were also found in higher levels. The second unit, 4000 B.C. to after 3000 B.C., has waisted blades and flaked and polished lenticular-section axe-adze blades. At this level pig bone was also found. The top cultural level began sometime after 3000 B.C. and contains polished axe-adze blades with a planilateral cross-section and three fragments of undecorated pottery (Bulmer and Bulmer, 1964).

Yuku Rockshelter in the Western Highlands district (Map 4) had pebble and flake tools, including large thickly-backed scrapers, associated with waisted blades at its lowest levels. Above these were ground lenticular-section axe-adzes and waisted blades with ground edges. The top levels contained small flake tools and planilateral ground axe-adze fragments. A date of about 9780 ± 150 B.P. has been obtained for the upper deposit of Yuku (Bulmer and Bulmer, 1964; Bulmer, 1964; Allen, 1972b).

The Niobe Rockshelter in the Chimbu District (Map 4) had pebble and flake tools, a horse-hoof-like core, two partially ground waisted blades, and a number of flaked and ground lenticular-section axe-adze blades. The site is undated and the stratification unclear, but the waisted blades predate polished axe-adzes. A considerable quantity of dog, pig, and hen bones was excavated (White, 1965).

The Batari Rockshelter in the Eastern Highlands district (Map 4) lacked waisted blades and pebble tools. Flaked scrapers and waisted flakes

were found in abundance.[3]   A complex of hearths
containing pig bones extended over the excavated
unit just below the surface.   Dates from below the
hearth complex indicate an occupation starting
sometime before 6000 B.C.   No evidence of pig was
found in this lower part of the deposit (White,
1969, p. 29).

Aibura Rockshelter, also in the Eastern Highlands district (Map 4), had flake tools.   Associated
with these in upper levels were ground axe-adzes
blades of lenticular and planilateral cross-sections,
pig and dog bones, and eighteen sherds of pottery that
date to less than 1000 years ago (Allen, 1972b).

The earliest definite evidence of agriculture
in the highlands comes from two sites in the Wahgi
Valley in the Western Highlands district.   The
Manton Site (Map 4) revealed an extensive system
of agricultural drainage ditches associated with
fence posts, digging sticks, a paddle-shaped spade,
ground stone axe-adze blades, and grinding stones.
These remains are certainly the result of a well-
developed agricultural system, and must have been
preceded by a long period of food production.   One
digging stick was dated at 350 B.C.   A second
radiocarbon date of 2650 B.C. appears to predate
agriculture in the immediate area (Golson, Lampert, Wheeler, and Ambrose, 1967; White, 1971).
Very similar material was found at the Kuk Site:
extensive ditches, pointed digging sticks, paddle-
shaped spades, fence posts, a bow, and ground axe-
adze blades (mostly planilateral in section),
grinding stones, and clubheads.   Two unusual types
of artifacts found were a bipointed ground stone
knife and a large tanged flaked hoe resembling
some of the earlier waisted blades.   House mounds
and evidences of house floors were also found at
the Kuk Site (Allen, 1972b; Golson, 1974).

Though archaeology is new in New Guinea and
excavated sites are few, one can speculate about
the possible course of events in the highlands.
There was an initial occupation of New Guinea during the Pleistocene. The earliest date for this
šo far is about 25,000 B.C., and as in the case of
Australia, once simple watercraft were available
to man the initial occupation could have been made
readily during times of glacial maxima. Evidence
of early settlement comes only from the highlands.
This may be due to the paucity of archaeological
surveys and excavations in the lowlands and to the
fact that areas where early sites might have
existed on the Sahul Shelf are now covered by sea
water. The pebble and flake tools are amorphous
and difficult to compare to other stone industries.
They are, however, similar to early lithic material found both in Australia and in Southeast
Asia. Unifacially worked pebble tools are, for
example, found in all areas. The horse-hoof core
from Niobe Rockshelter is a common Australian
type, and highland New Guinea saw an early use of
ground stone tools and waisted blades. Very early
edge-ground axes are also found in the Oenpelli
area of Arnhem Land and waisted blades have been
found on the surface in New Britain.
Lenticular axe-adzes, both flaked and ground,
seem to have been followed by ground axe-adzes of
planilateral cross-section. New Guinea flake
types are nondescript and seem to defy traditional
schemes of classification. However, from most ancient times to the present, the lithic industries
display a remarkable lack of change. Though new
tool types and new forms of subsistence are introduced, many earlier tool types continue unchanged.

The agriculture of New Guinea and other Pacific Islands is based on the cultivation of root crops such as yam and taro, and tree crops such as banana, breadfruit and coconut, and sugar cane. In New Guinea the legume Pueraria is also grown and may have been an ancient cultigen. With the possible exception of sugar cane, which may be native to New Guinea, the rest of the crops, together with domestic pig and chicken, are Asiatic in origin. These tropical crops are not well suited to the cool climate of highland New Guinea, and today the sweet potato of South American origin introduced not more than 400 years ago is the major crop. The finds in the Wahgi Valley indicate, however, that elaborate agricultural techniques were established in the highlands by 350 B.C. before the introduction of the sweet potato.

When and how food production began in New Guinea remain unknown. Evidence from Southeast Asia suggests the possibility of early experimentation with plant cultivation in that area. The first inhabitants of the highlands probably were hunters and gatherers finding an abundance of plant, marsupial, and bird life. Attempts at food production may have occurred independently in New Guinea or may have been part of the subsistence activities brought to the island by early migrants. The presence of both axe-adzes and waisted blades (which may have functioned as hoes) seems to indicate exploitation of plant resources for at least 10,000 years. Further excavations and collection and quantitative analysis of faunal and floral remains are badly needed. The presence of pig bone by 4500 B.C. probably indicates food production somewhere in New Guinea by that date, since domesticated pigs are dependent on cultivated food (Bulmer, 1966, pp. 504-505). The bones found may

well represent feral pig, but pigs are not native
to New Guinea and must have been brought to the
island by man as a domesticated, or at least tame,
animal.
     Pottery in the highlands is rare even today,
and the few sherds present at Kiowa and Aiturbi
Rockshelters may indicate trade with outside people. Marine shells found in the earliest levels
of highland archaeological sites may indicate long-
standing trade with coastal people. Though it is
possible that highland people went to the coast
and back to collect shell, it is more likely that
the shells were obtained from lowland people.

LOWLANDS

Very little archaeological work has been done in
coastal areas of Papua-New Guinea. Excavations at
the Nebira 4 site on the south coast of Papua (Map
4) and at Yule Island just off the central Papuan
coast revealed a fine red-slipped pottery decorated with incised and dentate stamp designs, some
filled with lime. The pottery is reminiscent of
the widespread Lapita pottery of Melanesia and
Polynesia. Radiocarbon dates obtained on the Nebira 4 materials indicate an occupation of the
site between A.D. 1 to A.D. 1000 or 1100. There
is evidence of gardening, of domesticated pigs and
dogs, and of hunting and fishing. Small flake
tools (e.g., blades, borers, and microcores) were
also found. These types of tools have not been
discovered in the highlands and do not resemble
tools of the Small Tool Tradition of Australia.
Allen (1972b) speculates that there may have been
an extensive culture settled on the south coast of
Papua correlated to the spread of Austronesian
languages at about 1000 B.C. to this area.

On the north coast at Wanigela at the head of
Collingwood Bay (Map 4), three excavated mounds
indicate an occupation by farming people who also
hunted and gathered shellfish between A.D. 420 and
1680.   Domestic pig and dog bones were found along
with incised and punctate decorated pottery and
ground stone axe-adze blades.   Pottery collected
from the surface around Collingwood Bay and in the
Trobriand Islands indicates trade relations between these areas in the prehistoric past.
On the small coral Tami Islands eight miles
off the northeast coast of the Territory of New
Guinea, archaeological investigations reveal axe-
adze blades of oval cross-section, obsidian flakes,
and potsherds.   The deposits are unstratified and
appear to be recent.   The pottery and sherds appear to be locally made, and the variety of pottery types found displays resemblances to the modern pottery made at various villages in the area
today.
The western half of the island of New Guinea
is virtually unknown archaeologically.   Because of
the proximity of West Irian to the islands of
Southeast Asia, it is probable that this area has
archaeological sites that will be important in
answering the question of how man, his domestic
animals, and his cultivated plants reached New
Guinea.   Imported bronze tools and copies of them
have been reported from West Irian (de Bruijn,
1962).   Further investigations are needed to as-
say the amount and kind of influence Southeast
Asia may have had on the development of culture
in New Guinea.

ISLAND MELANESIA

Island Melanesia, lying both northeast and southeast of New Guinea, contains evidence important

for understanding the spread of peoples throughout
Oceania.   On New Britain in the Bismarck Archipelago waisted blades similar to those from older
sites in New Guinea have been found.   Lapita-style
pottery has been recovered from sites all the way
from the New Guinea coastline through Island Melanesia east to sites in western Polynesia.   This
pottery has been dated as far back as 2000 B.C.
Contemporaneous with the Lapita Pottery Tradition,
evidence has been uncovered of other pottery traditions on some islands (e.g., Buka and Sohano on
Buka Island, paddle-impressed on the Ile des Pins
and Fiji, and incised in Fiji and the New Hebrides).   Eventually we should be able to establish
cultural sequences in Melanesia based on pottery
traditions.   Obsidian found at widely separated
places has led to speculation about widespread
trading networks.

     The Trobriands, D'Entrecasteaux, Woodlark,
and Louisiade Islands off the eastern end of New
Guinea (Map 4) are virtually unknown archaeologically.   Site surveys in the Trobriands have revealed old village sites frequently located near
modern villages, arrangements of large standing
stones, and caves containing pottery, human bones,
and large seashells.   The sherds resemble pottery
from Wanigela at Collingwood Bay and that made in
the D'Entrecasteaux Islands, and it has been suggested that large trade networks are at least 1000
years old in this area (Egloff, 1971).

     Nuamata is a small island, now uninhabited,
off Goodenough Island in the D'Entrecasteaux
group.   This island was used as a burial site.   A
large number of jars containing human skeletal remains were found, and the pottery resembles that
from the Collingwood Bay area and the D'Entrecasteaux Islands (Egloff, 1972).

Bismarck Archipelago. The Bismarck Archipelago
has at present only a few reported sites. In the
Kandrian area of New Britain (Map 4), Chowning and
Goodale collected about 300 percussion flaked
tools (Goodale, 1966). Made of local cherts, the
tools include bipointed blades, waisted blades,
flake scrapers, core-bifaces, and axe-adze blades
(see Fig. 6, next page). Though these materials
were found on the surface and cannot be dated,
they appear to be very ancient. The waisted
blades are similar to those described from older
sites in New Guinea. The industry may represent
the movement of people off New Guinea to New Britain in Late Pleistocene or early Holocene times
(Shutler and Kess, 1969; Golson, 1971a).

LAPITA POTTERY TRADITION

Lapita-style pottery has attracted much interest
because of its widespread distribution, its antiquity, and the possibility that it may be part
of a cultural complex from which Polynesian culture arose. Sites at which Lapita pottery has
been found range from western Melanesia to western
Polynesia (Map 1). Lapita pottery is named from
the site of that name in New Caledonia, excavated
by Gifford and Shutler in 1951. Radiocarbon dates
for these pre- and proto-Polynesian occupation
sites range from ca. 2000 B.C. to the beginning of
the Christian era (see Table 2, p. 59). The
Lapita-ware makers lived along the shore, and were
fishermen and shellfish eaters. In the beginning
they appear to have been reef exploiters with no
clear evidence, as yet, of horticulture. Later in
their history they acquired pigs and food plants
such as yams, taro, and bananas.

Fig. 6.   Kandrian area artifacts, New Britain.
(a) bipointed blade; (b) waisted blade; (c) flaked
scraper; (d) core-biface; (e) axe-adze (after
Shutler and Kess, 1969).

TABLE 2.   Lapita Pottery Sites and Dates

Site	Location	C-14 date
Watom	Watom Island, Bismarck Archipelago	500 B.C.?
Ambitle	Ambitle Island, Bismarck Archipelago	?
Yule Island	Hall Sound	100 B.C.?
Gawa	Reef Islands, Solomon Islands	1005 & 825 B.C.
Sohano	Buka Island, South Bougainville	500 B.C.
Talasea area	New Britain	?
North Coast, Bougainville	Bougainville	?
Lapita, Site 13	New Caledonia	845 B.C.
Vao	Ile des Pins, New Caledonia	905 B.C.
Vatcha	Ile des Pins, New Caledonia	2190 B.C.
Erueti	Efate, New Hebrides	350 B.C.
Avunatari	Malo, New Hebrides	70 B.C.
Aore	New Hebrides	1300 B.C.
Natunuku	Viti Levu, Fiji	1290 B.C.
Yanuca Island	Viti Levu, Fiji	1030 B.C.
Sigatoka	Viti Levu, Fiji	510 B.C.
To 2	Tonga	1140 B.C.
Tunuga	Tonga	?
Upolu	Samoa	800 B.C.?

In 1909, Meyer (1909, 1910) excavated some pottery of distinctive decorations, later identified as Lapita, on Watom Island, four miles off

the northeastern tip of New Britain.   In 1965,
Specht (1968) reopened excavations on Watom and
found both plain and decorated sherds, ranging in
color from red to brown to grey to black.   Some of
the decorated sherds had a red slip, and the pottery was tempered with shell, sand, and grit.   The
designs were made by dentate stamping, nail impressions, linear incisions, and applied relief (see
Fig. 7, p. 62, for similar motifs).   Several shell
rings, obsidian flakes, polished axe-adze blades
of lenticular cross-section, and flat basalt
flakes with ground edges were also found.   A series of radiocarbon dates indicate that the occupation started before 470 B.C.   Before A.D. 1250 a
volcanic eruption left a layer of ash over the island and the area was reoccupied by people who did
not have pottery.   They appear to be the ancestors
of the present inhabitants, the Tolai, who also
lack pottery.
      Ambitle Island (Map 4) off the southeast
coast of New Ireland is another place in the Bismarck Archipelago where Lapita pottery has been
found.   The sherds come from buried deposits and
were associated with a few obsidian flakes.   The
sherds closely resemble those of Watom Island
(White and Specht, 1973).   The obsidian flakes
found with the Lapita pottery on both Watom and
Ambitle may come from Talasea (Map 4) on the Wil-
lamuez Peninsula of New Britain.   Recently Lapita
pottery has been found on Gawa in the Reef Islands
(Map 4) of the Santa Cruz group of the Solomon Islands.   Here again obsidian flakes were associated
with the sherds.   Radiocarbon dates of 1000 B.C.
and 825 B.C. were obtained.   Ambrose and Green
(1972) claim that emission spectrography shows
that the Ambitle and Gawa obsidian flakes are
indistinguishable and originated from the same

source, Talasea. From Talasea, Watom is 270 km.,
Ambitle is 500 km., and Gawa is 2000 km. This
evidence of long-distance travel and possible
trade in the first millenium B.C., if valid, argues for considerable maritime skill on the part
of the people involved.[4]

   Red-slipped, sand-tempered pottery bearing relief and incised decoration, is reported from Lesu
in northern New Ireland with a radiocarbon date of
500 B.C. This pottery is somewhat like Lapita pottery, and may be related not only to Lapita but
also to the red-slipped pottery reported along the
south coast of New Guinea. Large numbers of marine shells, some fish and pig bones, Tridacna
shell axes, shell arm rings, small obsidian flakes,
and slingstones were also found. At Balof Cave on
New Ireland, sherds resembling those found at Lesu
and bone points and obsidian flakes were found in
the upper cultural level. Below this, pottery was
absent, and a flaked stone industry, mostly of unretouched flakes of chert and volcanic rock, was
found. A few flaked artifacts resembled similar
specimens in New Guinea. These layers may date to
about 6000 years ago (White, 1972).

   Tanged flakes, waisted and unwaisted blades
similar to those of New Guinea and New Britain,
have recently been reported from South Bougainville (Nash and Mitchell, 1973). Specht's (1969)
surveys and excavations on Buka Island (Map 4) led
him to describe a ceramic complex that started
about 500 B.C. and lasted until the present day.
Two pottery styles were found, the Buka and the
Sohano. The Buka pottery is composed of a crumbly
paste tempered with shell and sand. Some of it
has traces of a red slip. Vessel forms are mainly
shallow open bowls. Few sherds are decorated, but
those that are bear incised geometric designs, and
two sherds have dentate stamped decorations exactly

Fig. 7. Decorated Lapita sherds from Site 13, New Caledonia (Shutler).

like those of Lapita pottery. The paste of these vessels and those of Watom Island are almost identical. Sohano sherds were more numerous than Buka sherds. Sohano pottery, tempered with volcanic ash, appears to have been locally made and to be related stylistically to the Marianas plainware of Micronesia. Most Sohano vessel forms are shallow bowls decorated with rows of punctations, simple incised or relief designs. The stratigraphy of the two excavated sites is unclear. Buka sherds are most frequent at the lowest levels of the site in which a few Sohano sherds are also found. In higher levels, the Buka sherds are completely replaced by Sohano sherds. Two explanations are possible: first, that Buka style pottery precedes Sohano style; second, that both imported Buka pottery and locally made Sohano pottery were used in early times, but only Sohano pottery was used in later times (Specht, 1969).

During 1973, Specht located a number of sites in the Talasea area of west New Britain that included Lapita-style pottery in association with obsidian (Specht, 1973; Map 4). Specht (1969) also collected similar pottery during a site survey of the north coast of Bougainville Island nearest Buka. Archaeologically, Bougainville Island is otherwise unknown, and published results of a survey and excavations by John Terrell in 1969-1970 are awaited.

Solomon Islands. On Santa Ana Island, Davenport (1972) excavated three shallow caves that show the island to have been continuously occupied since before A.D. 150. Roger Green reexcavated one of

these sites and obtained a radiocarbon date of
about 1000 B.C. (Green, personal communication,
1973). There is some evidence of population increase during these times. The amount of shell
in the deposit indicates a greater reliance on
shellfish than at present. Small blades of chal-
cedony resembling those reported from New Britain
by Chowning and Goodale (1966), thermally fractured volcanic cooking stones, and shell artifacts
similar to those used today were found. A crumbly
red pottery, thought to be related to Lapita pottery, was used between A.D. 140 and 670. It was
found only in very small quantities. Pottery is
not now made on Santa Ana, and the few sherds
found may have been imported.

On Guadalcanal at the Poho Valley site, Davenport (1968) excavated twelve feet of stratified
deposits lacking any evidence of ceramics. Some
of the artifacts found are somewhat different than
those found on Santa Ana, and a radiocarbon date
of 970 B.C. demonstrates that Guadalcanal has been
occupied for 3000 years.

A surface collection of flaked axe-adze
blades of various cross-sections, and a few highly
polished lenticular axe-adzes are reported from
Malaita. The present-day people claim that their
ancestors did not make the polished blades (Ross,
1970).

Although the results of Roger Green's work in
the Solomons have not yet been fully published,
the discovery of Lapita pottery associated with
simple obsidian flake tools on Gawa in the Reef
Islands has been announced. The material has two
radiocarbon dates of 1000 and 825 B.C. (Ambrose
and Green, 1972).[5]

New Caledonia. In 1952, Gifford, assisted by the
authors, conducted an archaeological survey in New

Caledonia.   Eleven sites were chosen for test excavations, and results of this work from ten of the
sites showed that the historic cultural patterns
of the New Caledonia began at least by A.D. 150
and probably earlier.   The people were farmers who
also fished and gathered shellfish.   The brown pottery similar to that made in New Caledonia in historic times is paddle- and anvil-finished and has
incised decorations of lines, gouges and gashes,
relief nubbins, ribs and cross-hatching, and ap-
pliqued designs.   Shell net sinkers, fishhooks,
bracelets, beads, and paring knives also resemble
objects used in historic times.   Axe-adze blades
of lenticular cross-section, chisels, bipointed
sling stones, flat disc-shaped ceremonial maces,
and beads were made of ground stone.   Anomalous
flake scrapers were present but not common (Gifford and Shutler, 1956).

At the Lapita site (Site 13) on the Foué Peninsula (Map 4), Lapita-style pottery was found
(Fig. 7).   The site had been used as a yam field,
and the deposit had been turned over.   As a result
of cultivation, the Lapita pottery was found mixed
with the non-Lapita pottery previously described.
Subsequent examination of the area by the authors
showed in places a stratum bearing only Lapita
sherds.   A radiocarbon date of 847 B.C. shows the
Lapita occupation here to be at least that old.
Because of the disturbed nature of the deposit, it
is not clear what other artifacts were associated
with the sherds.

Work by Smart (Golson, 1968) on beach sites
north of Noumea disclosed an early phase with
paddle-impressed pottery, followed by a thick ware
with horizontal handles.   The upper level has pottery with relief and incised decorations.   Radiocarbon dates of 115 B.C. for the paddle-impressed

pottery, A.D. 205 for pottery with handles, and
A.D. 315 for pottery with handles and incised
decoration were obtained (Shutler, 1971). Lapita
pottery also has been found at Vao on the Ile des
Pins (Map 4) off the southeast coast of New Caledonia. Here Lenormand (1948) excavated a midden
on the coast cut by sea erosion. Further excavations took place on the Ile des Pins in 1949 and
1960 (Golson, 1962), and a date of 905 B.C. was
obtained from an area near the bottom of the occupation. A nearby site, Vatcha (Map 4), has been
excavated (Frimigocci, 1970a and 1970b), and large
pieces of Lapita pottery, hearths, cooking stones,
and ancient form of bulimus shell, shell, and
turtle and fish bone were found. A radiocarbon
date of 2190 to 2030 B.C. was obtained. This is
the earliest date so far recorded in association
with Lapita pottery.

On the Ile des Pins arrangements of over 400
conical tumuli have been found on the central
plateau. Similar tumuli also have been found on
the "Grande Terre," the mainland of New Caledonia
near Paita. The tumuli of iron-oxide gravel on
the Ile des Pins average about 2½ meters high and
have a diameter of 10-15 meters. They are clearly
man-made but completely unknown to the present-day
people. They do not seem to be associated with
habitation sites. Chevalier (1962) has sectioned
some of these tumuli and found they contained an
inner cylinder 1 to 2 meters in diameter and 1 to
2.5 meters high made of hard lime mortar in which
shells have been found. No artifacts or charcoal
have been found in them. As perplexing as these
strange tumuli are, radiocarbon dates of mortar
and shells from three tumuli near Paita are even
more astonishing. The dates are 5120 B.C., 7650
B.C., and 10,950 B.C. (Radiocarbon Dates Associ-

ates, Inc., 1966). Although evidence may well be
found someday indicating an early prehorticultural
occupation of New Caledonia, these dates may result from the use of dead coral and its associated shells to make lime.

Burial caves, stone alignments in the interior of the Grande Terre, petroglyphs, and extensive agricultural terraces are also seen in New
Caledonia. While their features have been recorded in large numbers, they have not yet been
identified with any specific prehistoric culture.

New Hebrides. Garanger's (1972) work in the central New Hebrides (Map 4) has revealed four ceramic traditions. On several sites on Makura,
Tongoa and Efate, an incised and relief decorated
pottery was found. Two kinds of pottery dating to
645 B.C. have been distinguished: Early Mangaasi
and Late Mangaasi. Paddle-impressed pottery (similar to Fijian paddle-impressed pottery) was collected from the surface of the Mele plain on Efate.
This pottery has not been found in stratigraphic
context in the New Hebrides. Pottery with internal incised designs appears at about 1000 A.D. at
the site of Aknau on Tongoa. Though this is the
only type found at the Aknau site, it sometimes
occurs in limited amounts with Late Mangaasi pottery at other sites on Tongoa and Makura. Lapita
pottery was found at the Erueti site on Efate, together with Mangaasi sherds and Tridacna shell
adzes similar to those of Tongoa. A date of 350
B.C. was obtained at this site.

Pottery disappeared from archaeological sites
on Tongoa before the violent volcanic eruption of
1400 A.D., and when the island was reinhabited,
pottery was no longer made. Pottery had also
disappeared in pre-European times on the other
islands of the central New Hebrides, probably

between A.D. 1300 and A.D. 1400. Garanger (1972)
speculates that the abandonment of the potter's
craft may be due to the arrival of new people coming by canoe from the south. These new people are
known from traditions and legends about the great
chief Roymata, whose elaborate burial with human
sacrifices was excavated by Garanger at Retoka Island near Efate. The burial was dated at A.D.
1265.

At Malo Island near Espiritu Santo in the
northern New Hebrides, Lapita sherds were found in
a mound at the Avunatari site by Hedrick (1971).
Petrographic analysis (Dickinson, 1971) indicates
that some of the sherds could not have been made
on Malo, but may have come from New Caledonia or
Papua. The sherds were associated with shell artifacts and thermally fractured rock. Two radiocarbon dates of 70 B.C. and A.D. 1010 have been puzzling. Hedrick has recently completed further
excavations on Malo and reports (personal communication) that the Avunatari mound is actually a
post-Lapita construction that incorporated lower-
level deposits containing Lapita pottery. This
finding explains the puzzling late A.D. 1010 date
for Lapita on Malo. Hedrick's recent excavations
on Malo and nearby Aore Island have produced a
large number of Lapita sites with obsidian flakes,
shell tools, stone adzes, and a variety of faunal
materials dating to about 1300 B.C.

The authors have located numerous archaeological remains from surveys on the larger islands of
the northern New Hebrides (Map 4). Red-slipped
pottery is abundant on Espiritu Santo and still is
made on the west coast (Shutler, 1968). Incised
wares from Malekula and Aobe were also recovered.
Small mounds, some of them rubbish heaps, are reported from some sites on Santo and Malekula.
Malekula has an abundance of pottery-bearing sites,

with a large number of design motifs (see Fig. 8,
next page). In the southern islands of the New
Hebrides (Map 4), Tanna, Aniwa, Futuna, and Aneityum, very little pottery has been found, and no
pottery has been made there in historic times.
Radiocarbon dates show that Tanna was inhabited by
at least 420 B.C., Futuna (a Polynesian outlier)
by A.D. 300, and Aneityum by at least A.D. 1100.
Stone and shell artifacts show considerable similarity from island to island in the New Hebrides.
Polished stone axe-adze blades are lenticular or
oval in cross-section and seem always to be rare
(see Fig. 9, p. 72). Tridacna, Conus, and Terebra
shell adzes are much more common (see Fig. 10, p.
74). Mitra chisels, vegetable peelers (usually
Cypraea tigris), choppers and scrapers made of
heavy shell, stone abraders, and rubbing stones
are known (see Fig. 11, p. 76), and long cylindri-
cal clubs are found on Tanna and Futuna. A variety of shell beads, pendants, and bracelets are
also reported (Shutler and Shutler, 1965, 1967;
see Fig. 12, p. 78).

Fiji. Gifford's (1951) pioneer work on Viti Levu
in the Fiji Islands (Map 4) yielded a cultural sequence that has been revised by Green (1963). The
Sigatoka Phase is characterized by Lapita pottery
from a number of sites (Gifford, 1951). The earliest date, 1290 B.C., comes from the Natunuku
site in northwest Viti Levu; the Yanuca Island
site has an early date of 1030 B.C. and the Sigatoka site, 510 B.C. All are associated with Lapita pottery (Shutler, 1971). At Sigatoka, stone
flakes, polishers, and two axe-adze blades with
rectangular, plano-convex cross-section were associated with the pottery.
      The Navatu Phase (which follows the Sigatoka
Phase) has paddle-impressed pottery. At the

Fig. 8.   Decorated sherds from Malekula, New Hebrides (Shutler).

Navatu and Vunda sites, it lasted from 100 B.C. to A.D. 1100 (Shaw, 1967). At the Yanuca Island site, excavated by the Birks, paddle-impressed pottery is associated with a date of 710 B.C. (Shutler, 1971). At Sigatoka the Navatu Phase seems to be represented by paddle-impressed pottery, flat-bottomed dishes with mat and leaf impressions, and axe-adze blades of lenticular cross-section.

The subsequent Vunda Phase has large amounts of plain pottery and some incised sherds. At the Vunda site the phase seems to begin at about A.D. 1250, and it lasted until A.D. 1643 (Shaw, 1967). The final Ra Phase, beginning with initial European contact, is marked by an increase in incised sherds. Numerous fortified sites, described as "ring ditch," have been reported from Fiji. Ring ditch sites have a mound surrounded by a circular ditch and bank system, crossed at points with causeways. Enormous numbers of ring ditch sites have been found on Viti Levu, mainly on the windward side, and also on Wakaya Island. On ridge tops, more linear arrangements of banks and ditches are called "ridge forts." These, too, are reported from both Viti Levu and Wakaya. On Wayaka Island, three ridge forts had paddle-impressed pottery, which suggests that at least some of them may date to the Navatu Phase. Both forms of forts were in use at the time of European contact (Gifford, 1951; Palmer, 1967, 1969).

Several problem areas are becoming clearly defined by recent archaeological work in Island Melanesia. The flint artifacts from New Britain and the flaked stone industry, lacking a pottery

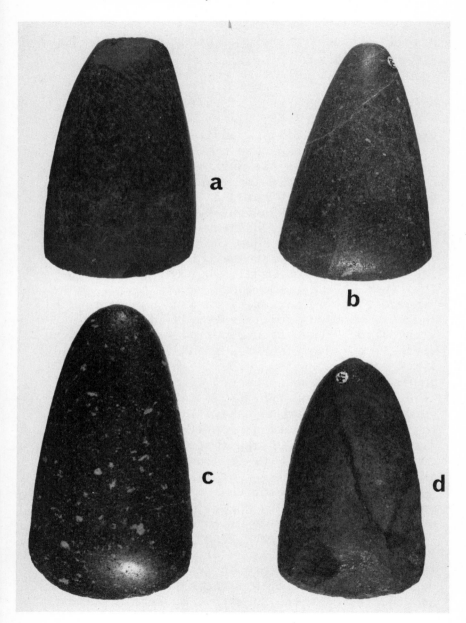

Fig. 9.   Stone axe-adzes from Pentecost, New Hebrides.   (a) adze; (b) axe; (c) axe; (d) adze
(Shutler).

association, found below pottery-bearing levels on
New Ireland, and similar artifacts from Bougainville strongly suggest an early occupation of
these islands.   This occupation may have been nonagricultural, as well as aceramic.   The New Guinea
highlands have evidence of farming but nonpottery-
using people.   If the first inhabitants of New
Britain and New Ireland were nonagricultural, it
is unlikely that they penetrated the smaller islands of Melanesia, where the comparative lack of
resources would have made hunting and gathering
difficult, if not impossible.   These stone industries may be connected with the spread of Papuan
speakers to these islands of western Melanesia.
      Various questions surround the role of Lapita
pottery in Melanesia.   It is not clear whether it
represents a type of pottery spread widely throughout Melanesia by migration, diffusion, trade, or
all three, or whether it represents a whole culture.   Unfortunately, at most Lapita sites, material remains other than ceramics are poorly represented.   In western Melanesia, a whole series of
Lapita sites are now known from the coast to New
Guinea, New Ireland, Buka, and Bougainville.   Like
the eastern Melanesian Lapita pottery sites, their
coastal orientation is consistent.   It is tempting
to view Lapita and similar pottery as evidence of
the rapid spread of Austronesian-speaking seagoing
farmers.   However, there is no conclusive evidence
that the Lapita people were farmers.   The fate of
this kind of pottery in Melanesia is quite unknown.
It may have been replaced by new kinds of pottery

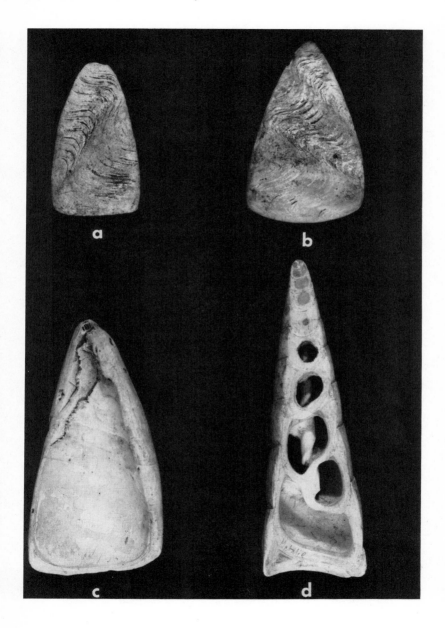

Fig. 10.   Shell adzes from Emau, New Hebrides.
(a-b) Tridacna; (c) Conus; (d) Terebra (Shutler).

brought by new people or simply altered into other
types.   The evidence from Buka, from the New Hebrides, and from Fiji suggests that both processes
took place.
     The elaborate Mangaasi pottery of the New
Hebrides has parallels in Fiji and New Caledonia.
Paddle-impressed pottery is known from Fiji, Ile
des Pins, and New Caledonia.   These two and others
may represent other long-established and far-flung
pottery traditions.
     Melanesia (New Guinea) was occupied in late
Pleistocene times and there is every reason to ex-
pect that dates even earlier than 26,000 B.P. at
Kosipe will be forthcoming.   Other significant de-
velopments are the extensive systems of agricultural drainage ditches in the Wahgi Valley dating
to 350 B.C., and the variety of pottery complexes
emerging from the coastal and offshore islands of
New Guinea.
     In Island Melanesia there is some evidence
that New Caledonia may have been occupied in the
terminal Pleistocene or early Holocene times.
The rest of this region was occupied by between
3000 and 4000 years ago.
     A review of current Melanesian studies makes
it clear that Melanesian origins cannot be sought
at a particular place nor at a particular time in
history (Shutler and Shutler, 1967).   The people
of Melanesia are the result of an extremely old
and continuing flow of people from the Asiatic
mainland into the islands of the southwest Pacific.
During the latter part of their history they have,
in addition, maintained sporadic contact with

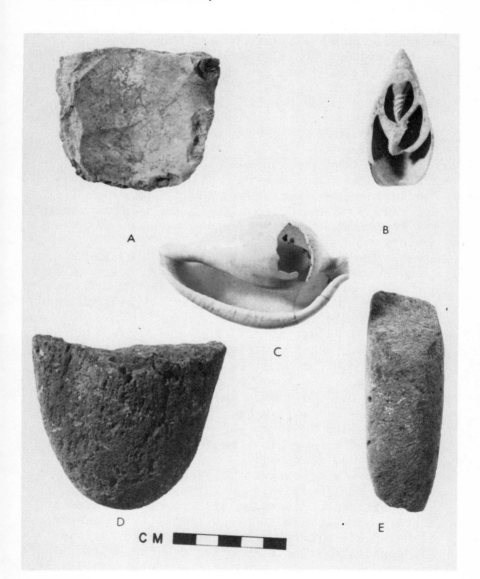

A B C D E

CM

Fig. 11. New Hebrides. (a) Tridacna scraper-chopper, Aneityum; (b) Mitra adze, Futuna; (c) Cyprea vegetable peeler, Futuna; (d) pumice abrader, Tanna; (e) coral file, Futuna (Shutler).

people inhabiting island groups to the north and east. From time to time and from many places, new movements of people have brought changes to the gene pools, to the languages and customs, and to the subsistence patterns of the people of the Melanesian islands. New ways of exploiting island environments continue to give impetus to movements within the island groups themselves and to further modify the life of the people. Shifting patterns of contact and isolation have brought and continue to bring other changes. Each new excavation brings something of this nature to light and, we suspect, will continue to do so.

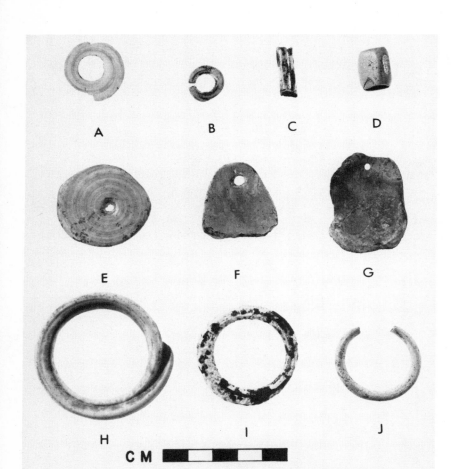

Fig. 12. New Hebrides. (a) incipient Conus shell
bead, Tanna; (b) Conus disk bead, Tanna; (c) bird
bone bead, Tanna; (d) pig tusk bead, Futuna; (e)
Conus shell pendant, Efate; (f) Pinctada shell pendant, Efate; (g) Ostrea shell pendant, Futuna; (h)
Conus shell pendant, Futuna; (i) Conus top ring
pendant, Futuna; (j) ring pendant, Futuna (Shutler).

Polynesia

The Hawaiian Islands in the north, Easter Island
in the east, and New Zealand in the south, comprise the three points of the Polynesian triangle.
Other major island groups in this huge expanse of
ocean are the Tongan and Samoan islands, the Society, Tuamotus, Cook, Tokelau, Ellice, and Marquesas Islands, and many more isolated ones (see Map
5, next page).

Both linguistic and archaeological data
clearly indicate that western Polynesia (Samoa and
Tonga, the Tokelau and Ellice Islands, Uvea and
Futuna; Map 5) was settled from somewhere in the
Fiji Islands or islands to the west, during the
second millennium B.C. (Garanger, 1972, p. 134;
Wurm, 1967). A series of excavations in Tonga
and Samoa (Davidson, 1969; Golson, 1959; Green
and Davidson, 1969; Groube, 1971; McKern, 1929;
Paulsen, 1967, 1968) have revealed the outline of
Polynesian origins and cultural development. The
rest of western Polynesia is virtually unknown
archaeologically.

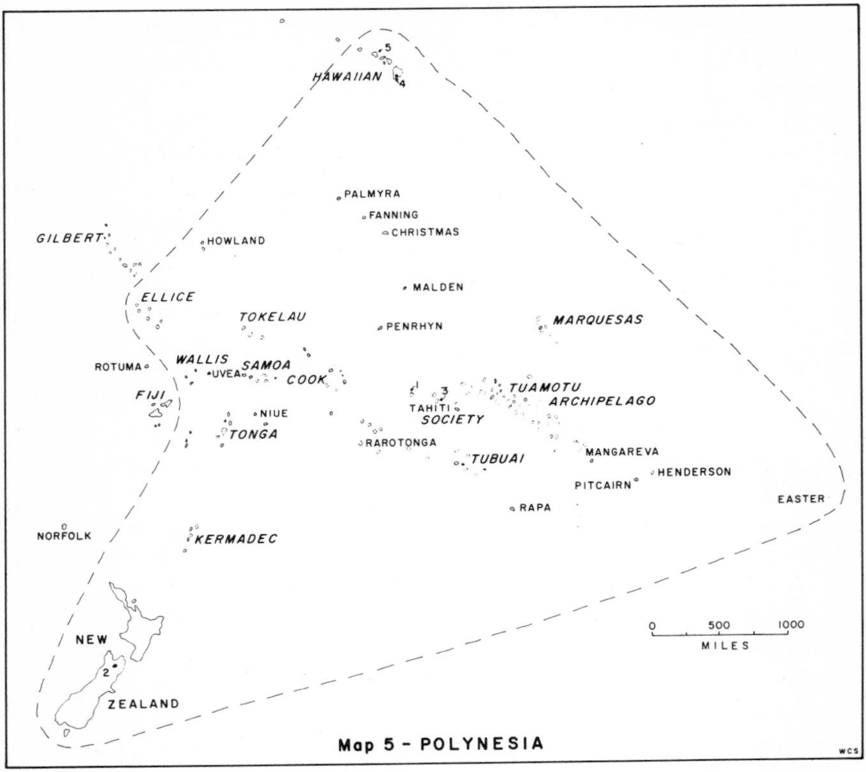

MAP 5.   Polynesia

1. Maupiti, Society
     Islands
2. Wairau Bar, New
     Zealand

3. Huahine, Society
     Islands
4. South Point, Hawaii
5. Bellows Beach, Hawaii

    Early radiocarbon dates of 1140 B.C. and 820
B.C. from a shell midden in Tonga are associated
with Lapita pottery remarkably similar to that of
Fiji (Groube, 1971). The ceramic tradition in

Tonga slowly changed from the highly differentiated and elaborate Lapita to a completely plain
ware by about 500 B.C. At a date as yet unknown,
perhaps early in the Christian era, pottery ceased
to be made in Tonga. The pottery reportedly used
in Tonga at the time of European contact seems to
have been trade ware from Fiji. Decorated Lapita
pottery has recently been found in Samoa dating to
possibly 800 B.C. This discovery makes Lapita pottery in Samoa of equivalent age to that of Tonga.
The suggested date of 800 B.C. for this style of
pottery in Samoa places Samoan pottery several hun-
dred years before the previously accepted time of
about A.D. 1. The significant aspect of the decorated Lapita pottery in Samoa is that it changes
the previously held idea of Tonga being the Polynesian homeland. Groube (1971, p. 313) "has suggested that it was in Tonga, in the first millennium B.C. that the Polynesian complex of physical
and cultural traits developed." Green argues on
the basis of the decorated Lapita pottery in Samoa
that ". . . changes in the pottery, adzes and
shell ornaments took place in Samoa as early as,
or earlier than, in Tonga. In short, it now appears that Samoa has an equal claim to be regarded
as a homeland in which Polynesian culture—though
not necessarily language—initially evolved"
(Auckland Star, July 1, 1973).
        Sites in Samoa containing exclusively plain
ware date from just before the first century B.C.
to the third century A.D. As in Tonga, pottery
making was abandoned sometime after that. Compar-
isons of adzes and shell artifacts suggest that in
other aspects of material culture the traditions
of Tonga and Samoa began to diverge from one another as well as from Fiji soon after the time of
initial settlement. This divergence in material

culture is reflected in recent linguistic classi-
fications, which divide Polynesian languages into
two subgroups: Tongic, which includes Tongan,
Niuean, and Uvean, and Nuclear Polynesian, which
includes Samoic and eastern Polynesian. Both
groups of Polynesian have Fijian as their nearest
relative (Pawley, 1972).

Groube (1971) has made the interesting suggestion that the makers of Lapita pottery were
"strandloopers" restricted to a shore environment
and exploiting mollusk resources from lagoons.
Pig bone has not yet been reported from Lapita
sites, and in Oceania the pig usually accompanies
horticulture. A growing population would have led
the Lapita people to adopt the food plants of
their horticultural neighbors to the west or to
have begun to place more reliance on food production, which may have been previously of little importance in their economy.

In any event, by the beginning of the Christian era Polynesian voyagers were ready to spread
their cultigens and domestic animals, plain pottery, and distinctive adze and house types to the
central islands of eastern Polynesia.

The earliest evidence of occupation in eastern Polynesia so far known comes from the Marquesas (Map 5). Excavations by Suggs (1961), Smith
(n.d.), and Sinoto and Kellum (Sinoto, 1970) have
established a four-phased scheme of cultural development for the Marquesas, originally postulated
by Suggs (1961) and considerably revised by Sinoto
(1968, 1970). Before the initiation of subsurface
archaeology in eastern Polynesia, the Society Islands were regarded as the probable immediate center of eastern Polynesian dispersals. Though the
archaeological evidence now points to the Marquesas instead, Bellwood (1970) has pointed out that

the Marquesas Islands have cliff-fringed coast and
narrow valleys with caves and rockshelters and
sandy beaches. These topographic features have al-
lowed a buildup of natural and cultural strata in
the Marquesas, while the Society Islands have few
cliffs and caves, and the more intensive agricultural activities on the coast may have destroyed
stratified natural and cultural deposits.

Sinoto dates the earliest phase of Marquesan
prehistory (Phase I Initial Settlement) at between
A.D. 300 and 600. The phase is characterized by a
maritime economy with an emphasis on hook and line
fishing, untanged and tanged adzes (Sinoto, 1970),
and plain pottery. It has been accepted by some
researchers on the basis of the adze, pottery, and
linguistic affiliations that this assemblage was
derived from Samoa. It has been demonstrated on
the basis of petrographic analysis that pots made
near Nasilai in the Rewa River Delta of Viti Levu,
Fiji, were transported to Tonga and on to the Marquesas. Sherds from these pots have been found on
Tungua, Tonga, and in the earliest site on Nuku
Hiva, NHaa 1. It seems probable that a group of
voyagers from Fiji, arriving in the Marquesas by
A.D. 300, were the discoverers of this group of
islands (Dickinson and Shutler, 1974). And since
Suggs has a date of ca. 130 B.C. from NHaa 1
(though its cultural context is not understood at
the present time), it seems reasonable to assume
that when this date is assigned to its proper cultural context, this pottery from Fiji, and therefore the date for the settlement of the Marquesas,
will be even earlier than A.D. 300. Phase II,
A.D. 600-1300, shows an increasing reliance on
food production probably associated with a growing
population. Changes in and elaborations of the
artifact inventory and the abandonment of pottery
making occurred during Phase III A.D. 1300-1600.

The earliest phases of occupation in the Society Islands (Map 5) are unknown. Burials on
Maupiti Island in the western part of the Society
group date to A.D. 860. Moreover the position of
the burials and their associated fishhooks, ornaments, and adzes are virtually identical with the
burials at Wairau Bar in New Zealand (Map 5), indicating the East Polynesian origin of New Zealand
culture (Emory and Sinoto, 1964). A wooden and a
whale bone patu of Chatham Island type discovered
on Huahine (Map 5) in the Society Islands by Sinoto comes from a cultural layer that may date as
early as A.D. 650 (Honolulu Star-Bulletin, 1973).
From the Marquesas and the Society Islands
Polynesian culture was carried to the far reaches
of the Polynesian triangle. Farthest to the east,
Easter Island (Map 5) was inhabited by A.D. 500.
This lonely island with its gigantic statues and
wooden tablets covered with the rongo rongo script
has attracted the attention of lovers of the mys-
terious and occult since its discovery, and the
origins of its people and culture have been as-
cribed variously to the Indus Valley, the Lost
Continent of Mu, and to ancient astronauts. More
prosaicly the inventories of artifacts in Easter
Island sites and linguistic parallels indicate
that Easter Island was settled by eastern Polynesians. The cool seas and fewer marine resources,
and the cool, rainy winters and hot, dry summers
led them to make cultural adaptations different
from those in the rest of eastern Polynesia.
Heyerdahl (1952, 1968) sought to derive the
culture of Easter Island and of the rest of Polynesia from the coast of British Columbia and
coastal South America, with minor additions of
food plants and domestic animals from Melanesia.
Linguistic evidence is solidly against this, and

the results of excavations in Melanesia and western Polynesia, especially the distribution of Lapita pottery and its appearance in early Polynesian contexts, offer further important evidence
against the possibility of an American center of
Polynesian origins. However, the presence of the
sweet potato, an American cultigen, in pre-European sites in eastern Polynesia, and its extreme
importance in both Easter Island and New Zealand
indicate Polynesian contact of some kind with
South America.

Hawaii, at the northern extreme of the Polynesian triangle (Map 5), also was first settled
from the Marquesas during the developmental phase
probably near A.D. 650. A series of sites at
South Point on the island of Hawaii (Map 5) and
from the Bellows Beach site on Oahu (Map 5) share
artifact similarities with each other and with
Phase II Marquesan material (Pearson, Kirch, and
Pietrusewsky, 1971; Emory and Sinoto, 1969). In
1970, a stratified sand dune site was excavated in
the Halawa Valley on Molokai. The first ovate
house form in the Hawaiian Islands was recorded
here. Radiocarbon dates provide a local sequence
of from A.D. 600-1200. The portable and nonport-
able artifacts indicate adaptation to a local environment, while close ties were retained with
other parts of east Polynesia (Kirch, 1971). Although other sites have been excavated in Hawaii,
unfortunately no general prehistoric sequence has
yet been established.

At the southern corner of the Polynesian triangle, New Zealand (Map 5) was occupied by A.D.
1000. As mentioned above, the similarities of
artifact types in early New Zealand sites with
the finds at Maupiti and Huahine in the Society
Islands indicate a Tahitian origin for Maori

culture.   Extensive and competent excavations in
New Zealand have revealed in broad outline the development of culture there.   Duff's (1956) original division of New Zealand prehistory into Moa
hunter and classic Maori has been revised and re-
fined.   Hypotheses that a "great fleet" introduced
Polynesian culture and horticulture, based pri-
marily on the sweet potato, to a non-Polynesian
fishing and hunting population have been disproved
(Sharp, 1957; Golson and Gathercole, 1962).   The
early Archaic (or Moa hunter) culture was first
established on North Island where the climate was
more favorable to tropical cultigens, and where
agriculture was practiced in earliest times.   The
rich avian and marine resources were not ignored,
however, and as the population spread south to
colder climates, hunting and gathering replaced
food production in some areas.   Adaptation to the
temperate climate and the large land mass of New
Zealand with its mineral resources, increasing reliance on cultivation of the sweet potato, and internal development in isolation from the rest of
Polynesia produced Maori culture in situ with some
items possibly coming from the Society Islands
(the Huahine patus).

The prehistory of other parts of eastern Polynesia is almost unknown.   Mangareva, at the eastern end of the Tuamotus (Map 5), was probably settled from the Marquesas about A.D. 1200 (Suggs,
1962); other parts of the Tuamotus seem to have
been settled from the Society Islands.   The Cook
and Austral Islands (Map 5) were also probably
settled from the Society Islands (Duff, 1959).
The importance of the Society Islands, together
with the Marquesas, as a center for dispersal of
east Polynesian culture makes the lack of early
excavated sites in Tahiti (Map 5) especially re-

grettable.   Recent work by Sinoto in southeast
Polynesia indicates that Pitcairn Island (Map 5)
was inhabited by A.D. 1335 ± 105 and Henderson Island (Map 5) by A.D. 1160 ± 100.   Sinoto suggests,
on the basis of adze types and other artifacts
found on these islands, that their first occupants
were from the Marquesas (Sinoto, personal communication, 1974).

Outlying Polynesian Islands.   One of the curious
features of the distribution of Polynesian people
in the Pacific is the presence of a number of
Polynesian populations living on small islands
scattered along the eastern edge of Melanesia and
Micronesia.   These people speak Polynesian languages and have some degree of Polynesian social
organization, while their economy and material culture show varying degrees of similarity with those
of their Melanesian and Micronesian neighbors.   In
1962, Capell suggested that these island populations represented groups left behind in a movement
of Polynesian speakers from Southeast Asia to
their present position in the Polynesian triangle.
The identification of Fiji as the place of Polynesian beginnings and a series of linguistic studies
(Bayard, 1966; Elbert, 1967, Green, 1971; Pawley,
1967) have shown that the outlying Polynesian populations, rather than having been left behind in
a west to east migration, represent a series of
different, later, east to west migrations from
western Polynesia.   Howells (1974) suggests that
this westward movement was from Samoa through the
Ellice Islands.
        Excavations on Futuna, a Polynesian outlier
in the southern New Hebrides (Map 4), tested a
series of rockshelters that were used as campsites,
storage areas, and burial places.   Radiocarbon

dates ranged between A.D. 310 and 1780 (Shutler
and Shutler, 1965; Shutler, 1971). The tools and
ornaments recovered closely resemble those of Melanesian groups in the southern New Hebrides. Pottery is lacking here as in the rest of the southern New Hebrides. Capell (1960) and the authors'
informants on Futuna report that in pre-European
times only chiefs were buried and the bodies of
other people were thrown into the sea. This fact
is not consistent with the number of burials of
men, women, and children found on Futuna.

Fila Island off the south coast of Efate (Map
4) is another Polynesian outlier in the New Hebrides. Here excavations yielded a great deal of
pottery, mostly plain but some with incised and
applique decorations similar to pottery from Malekula and Espiritu Santo. The modern people claim
never to have made or used pottery. It is possible that the archaeological deposits tested represent a pre-Polynesian occupation of Fila. Radiocarbon dates from the pottery bearing layers
ranged from A.D. 860 to A.D. 1135 (Shutler and
Shutler, 1965, 1968).

Excavations were made by Garanger (1972) on
yet another Polynesian outlier in the New Hebrides,
Mele (Map 4), which like Fila is a small islet off
the coast of Efate. Remains of house structures
and a series of burials indicate a late occupation
of the islet. A radiocarbon date of A.D. 1625
came from the bottom of the lowest level. The inhabitants of Mele did not use pottery and only one
sherd was found in the excavation, though pottery
is abundant in other archaeological sites on Efate.
Garanger suggests that the Polynesian population
was established on Mele after pottery had disappeared from the material cultural inventory of the
surrounding Melanesian people—probably sometime

between A.D. 1135 when pottery was being used on
Fila Island and A.D. 1625.

Further to the north in the Solomon Islands,
test excavations were conducted on Anuta (Map 4)
by Kirch and Rosendahl (1973). Here the present
Polynesian inhabitants have a culture similar to
that of Tikopia (Map 4). Lower levels of these
excavations contained quantities of plain pottery,
shell adzes, and fishhooks. The earliest date on
the pottery bearing levels is 880 B.C. and pottery
making seems to have been abandoned by about A.D.
500. The early date is surprising and at this
time inconsistent with the data from western Polynesia. Possibly these deposits, like those on
Fila Island, represent a pre-Polynesian occupation.

In Micronesia Davidson (1971) excavated on
Nukuoro (see Map 6, p. 91) a small atoll that is
one of two Polynesian outliers in the eastern Carolines. The island has been occupied since about
A.D. 1300. The importance of fishing in the island's economy is shown by the large number of
fishhooks and fish bones recovered. The first
settlers brought dogs with them, but these soon
died out. Pigs and chickens were first brought to
the island by Europeans. Various kinds of shell
adzes were found that are similar in type to those
reported from elsewhere in Micronesia and parts of
Melanesia.

Micronesia

Micronesia, whose islands are spread out over the central and northwest Pacific, is composed of four major groups of small islands, mostly coral atolls: the Gilbert, Marshall, Caroline, and Marianas islands (Map 6). Very little archaeological work has been done in Micronesia, almost all of it in the western part. Excavations in the Marianas, Yap, and Palau, and Davidson's work on Nukuoro (described above), represent the most extensive subsurface archaeology in eastern Micronesia.[6]

Marianas. The pioneering research of Spoehr (1957) on Saipan, Tinian, and Rota (Map 6) established the presence of two sequential culture periods in the Marianas: the pre-Latte and the Latte, defined by the presence or absence of Latte structures. Latte are double rows of capped, short, stone pillars that functioned as piling foundation of important houses. The pre-Latte period lacked these distinctive pilings and is characterized by Marianas redware pottery, and a lime-filled impressed ware (thought to be a trade ware), shell and stone adzes, shell beads and pendants (Spoehr, 1957),

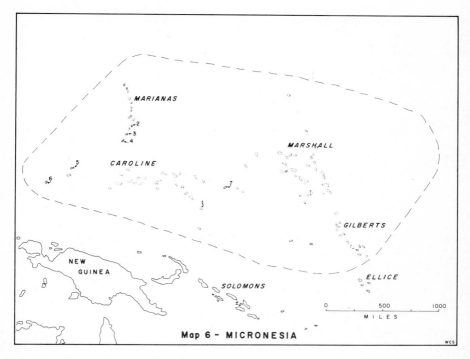

MAP 6.   Micronesia

1.   Nukuoro   5.   Yap
2.   Saipan   6.   Palau
3.   Rota   7.   Ponape
4.   Guam

and extended burials (Pellett and Spoehr, 1961).
This period is not well represented in excavations
and is as yet poorly known. A radiocarbon date
from Saipan indicates that pre-Latte began by 1527
B.C. The Latte period possessed the typical stone
foundations, Marianas plainware and various decorated variants, stone and shell adzes, stone mor-
tars and pestels, pounders, dishes, shell and bone

fishhooks, shell scrapers, and parers. Marianas
plainware resembles the Sohano from Buka in Melanesia. Spoehr's date indicates that the Latte period started by A.D. 845.

Excavations on Roto (Map 6) by Takayama and
Egami (1971) explored a Latte structure there.
Burials were found, some evidently contemporaneous
with the structure (A.D. 1640-1780) and some made
before the structure was built (A.D. 1335-1525).
The earlier burials were secondary interments with
the exception of three burials of children, all in
an extended position. The burials associated with
the Latte structure are thought to have been ex-
posed on the surface. Impressions of rice husks
on potsherds dating from A.D. 1335 indicate that
rice was cultivated in the Marianas prior to European discovery.

Reinman's (1968a) excavations on nearby Guam
(Map 6) showed the presence of the pre-Latte and
Latte periods on that island as well. Latte period sites were abundant, while the pre-Latte period
was represented only by scattered evidence in the
lower levels of excavated sites. The pottery of
Guam is similar to, though not identical with, the
pottery of Saipan, Tinian, and Rota. Both Marianas redware and plainware have been found. Radiocarbon dates obtained on Guam range from 1320 B.C.
to modern times (Reinman, 1968b).

Carolines. To the southwest of the Marianas, the
Giffords (1954) tested a number of sites on Yap
in the western Carolines (Map 6). Here no Marianas redware or other evidence of the pre-Latte
period was found. Two kinds of pottery was described: an earlier "unlaminated" pottery identical with Marianas plainware and a later "laminated"
pottery that is cruder, less well made, and un-
tempered. The "unlaminated" Marianas plainware

seems to have had a time span on Yap from at least
A.D. 176 to A.D. 847. Shell artifacts of types
found in the Marianas were abundant on Yap (Gifford and Gifford, 1959).

Osborne's (1958) excavations in the Palaus
(Map 6) indicate that these islands have been occupied for probably as long a time as the Marianas,
though no radiocarbon dates are available. Palauan pottery became thicker, coarser tempered, and
more poorly fired through time, as on Yap. Extensive agricultural terraces and large sites indicate a large population at times in the past.
Shell artifacts resemble those of the Marianas.
Trade beads indicate contact with Southeast Asia
as early as 200 B.C.

Davidson (1967) conducted preliminary archaeological investigations on Ponape (Map 6) and other
eastern Caroline Islands. On Ponape, stone structures with walled and unwalled burial sites were
recorded, as were stone or coral platforms, with
or without central pits, and varied numbers of
tiers and rectangular enclosures. Deep middens
are rare, and artifacts were mostly shell.

From Ponape, three radiocarbon dates, the
samples collected by Evans, Meggers, and Riesen-
berg in 1963 from ceremonial fires at Site P-2,
range from A.D. 1180 to A.D. 1430 (Radiocarbon,
1965).

The bulk of the shell artifacts in Micronesia
show a close resemblance to those of southern Melanesia. Similarly, on the basis of still rudimentary linguistic analysis, Grace (1964) has pos-
ited a relationship between some southern Melanesian languages and Micronesian languages (with the
exception of Chamorro and Palauan). More archaeological and linguistic work in Micronesia is needed
to clarify this suggested relationship.

Agricultural terraces, rice, and various trade items indicate that at least the Palaus and the Marianas remained in contact with Asia after the initial settlement (Solenberger, 1967). Takayama and Egami (1971) have suggested that similarities in fishing gear, slingstones, burial customs, and other traits between the Marianas and Japan indicate that Japanese fishermen visited these islands in prehistoric times.

Oceanic Prehistory in Perspective

By describing the form and shape of some of the
artifacts found at various Asian, Southeast Asian,
Australian, and Pacific sites, their age when
known, and, in some cases, where and how they ar-
rived at the place they were discovered, we have
attempted to throw some light on the story of human cultural development in Oceania. Only brief
mention has been made of what people looked like
at various times and places, since this evidence
is meager indeed. Known and supposed languages
spoken by these people also have been touched on
briefly. At this point, by way of recapitulation
and some speculation, we shall summarize what the
evidence contributes to the general view of prehistoric cultural development in Oceania.

    The origins of man's occupation of Oceania
began on the mainland and islands of Southeast
Asia. From the Djetis bed at Modjokerto, east
Java, comes the earliest dated fossil human bones
in Asia, a Homo erectus child (Pithecanthropus
modjokertensis) at 1.9 ± 0.4 million years by
potassium/argon. The appearance of fossils of

95

early Homo sapiens in Java and the fact that no
pre-Homo sapiens fossils have as yet been identified east of Sundaland indicate that the Wallace
and Weber lines (Map 2) were major barriers to the
early expansion of peoples into Oceania.

The late Pleistocene occupation of Australia
has been established, with its Core and Scraper
Tradition, the Small Tool Tradition, and its
22,000-year-old edge-ground axes. The ancestors
of the Australian aborigines have not been clearly
identified, though Wadjak Man in Java seems to be
a leading candidate. A unique feature of Australia's prehistoric cultural development is the lack
of agriculture and pottery making. Tasmania, apparently not occupied until about 8000 years ago,
never progressed beyond the Core and Scraper stage.

New Guinea, the largest island in Melanesia,
was, like Australia, occupied by late Pleistocene
times. It is an island of great cultural, human,
and linguistic differences, as evidenced in the
variations of normally statured peoples and highland pygmy groups, the great diversity of Austronesian and non-Austronesian languages, and the numerous archaeological complexes now known for the
island. The Pleistocene settlers of New Guinea
were hunters and gatherers. This means of subsistence was followed by the introduction of horticulture by 4500 B.C. The Wahgi District agricultural drainage ditches and related items dated to
350 B.C. are important for understanding agricultural development in the highlands. There is a
suggestion that some plants were domesticated independently in New Guinea (e.g., sugar cane), but
the major food plants undoubtedly came from Southeast Asia where there is evidence of food production back possibly as early as 10,000 B.C. Horticulture throughout most of the Pacific is based on

root crops (yams, taro, and, in New Guinea, sweet potatoes). Breadfruit and pandanus are the staples on some low-lying atolls found in Micronesia.

There is evidence of a pre-pottery, pre-agricultural stage in Island Melanesia. This evidence comes from New Britain, where undated but primitive stone tools similar to some reported from early highland New Guinea sites have been found, from New Ireland, and from New Caledonia, where radiocarbon dates on the order of 10,000 B.P. have been obtained.

Pottery plays an important role in tracing migrations and unraveling culture history in Melanesia, and it is likely that the ultimate cultural sequences developed for Melanesia will be based on pottery traditions. Three major pottery traditions are recognized in Melanesia: Lapita Ware, Incised Ware, and Paddle-impressed Ware. The earliest well-dated culture of Island Melanesia is the Lapita pottery tradition, whose sites are found spread throughout the area. In New Caledonia, a Lapita site on the Ile des Pins has been dated at 2000 B.C. In some places and at some times the Incised Ware and the Paddle-impressed Ware are contemporaneous with the Lapita Ware [e.g., Paddle-impressed Ware from the Ile des Pins, dated at 905 B.C. and in Fiji at 710 B.C., and Incised Ware on Fiji (1290 B.C.) and in the New Hebrides (645 B.C.)]. Although these three major pottery traditions were widely distributed and contemporaneous in some places, we cannot say at this time what the relationship was between them. The first claims for long-distance trading in the Pacific have been made for Melanesia, where 3000 years ago over a distance of 1500 miles, obsidian and perhaps Lapita pottery may have been exchanged for unknown items.

The problem of Polynesia origins is far from
solved. At the present time Fiji is credited with
being the homeland of the proto-Polynesians with
settlers going from Fiji to Tonga and Samoa. William Howells (1974) speculates that the pre-Poly-
nesians came into eastern Melanesia from south-
eastern Micronesia. This cannot be demonstrated
yet with hard evidence, but the idea cannot be
cast aside lightly. However, all evidence at the
present time is against earlier theories that held
that Polynesians moved as a group through Melanesia or Micronesia.

In Polynesia, the Lapita pottery makers were
the first inhabitants, arriving in Tonga from Fiji
by 1140 B.C. Pottery making in Polynesia was
given up sometime in the early centuries of the
Christian era. In Samoa the discovery of decorated Lapita pottery, dating perhaps as early as
800 B.C., seems to give Samoa an equal claim to
that of Tonga as being the cradle of Polynesian
culture. Linguistic evidence, and similar artifacts found in early sites of Samoa and the earliest site in the Marquesas, lend support to the
possibility that the first people to arrive in the
Marquesas, with pottery from Fiji, did come from
Samoa via Tonga. This movement of people and/or
artifacts (Fijian pottery) through Tonga and possibly Samoa, long after the original settlement of
these two island groups, suggests a continuing in-
fusion of Fijian influence into Polynesia over a
long period of time.

Within Polynesia it is evident that the two
accepted divisions of western and eastern Polynesia are justified, with the western (Tonga and
Samoa) being occupied first and eastern Polynesia
being settled from this western cradle of Polynesian culture, thereafter developing regional

variations of a recognizable eastern Polynesian
culture.

A recent discovery of significance to the development of eastern Polynesian cultural history
is the establishment of the Society Islands as being at least partly responsible for occupation of
New Zealand and the homeland for some classic
Maori style artifacts.

The Polynesian Outliers, once thought to have
been the remnants of eastward-moving Polynesians,
are now known to have resulted from western migrations from western Polynesia after the Polynesian
culture base had been established. These westward
movements are not well understood, but they could
have derived from Samoa through the Ellice Islands
out into Melanesia and southern Micronesia.

Micronesia remains archaeologically the least
known area of Oceania. With its geographical position close to Asia and Island Southeast Asia,
migrations and influences from these regions were
to be expected and appear to have occurred in fact
(pottery, etc.). The Marianas Islands were occupied by 3500 B.C., while Yap and Palau because of
their close proximity to Asia could have been settled earlier. Various lines of evidence, both
linguistic and archaeological, suggest that the
rest of Micronesia was settled at a later date.
However, this supposition is very tentative.

Our views on the times of the peopling of the
various parts of Oceania is diagrammed in broad
aspect in Table 3. Discoveries will continue that
will require constant revisions of ideas regarding
the time and routes used to settle various parts
of Oceania and the influences affecting the prehistoric cultural development in this vast area.

TABLE 3.   Probable Dates of Settlement of Island Southeast Asia and Oceania

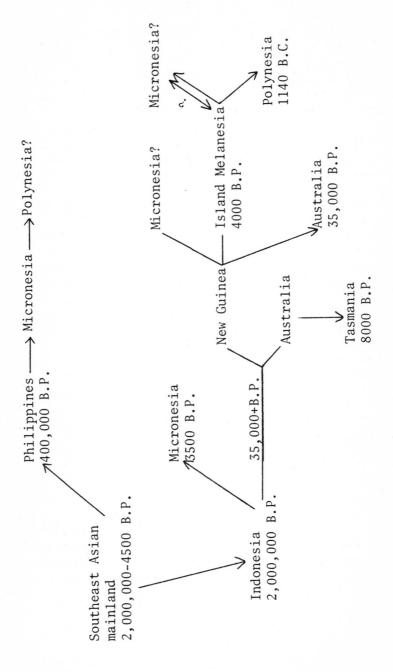

NOTES

1. There appear to be exceptions to this. Species of the marsupial cuscus, or phalanger, did reach Timor and the Celebes, and at least two species of stegodonts, a primitive group of elephants, somehow got from the Sunda Shelf to Flores and Timor, evolving into pygmy size. Apparently they came via the Philippines and the Celebes (Howells, 1974).

2. On the basis of this similarity, Coon (1962) has postulated a direct line of evolution leading from the Pithecanthropoid form of Homo erectus through Solo Man to Wadjak and the modern Australian aborigines. However, recent studies indicate that Solo Man is not related to aboriginal Australians and, in fact, ". . . the Solo crania may represent an extremely localized genetical dead-end which becomes extinct" (Macintosh, 1972, p. 1).

3. See Figs. 6(a) and 6(b) for waisted blades from the Kandrian area of New Britain, similar to those found at Kosipe, Kiowa, Yuku, Niobe, and Batari sites in the New Guinea highlands.

4. However, recent studies show that obsidian
signatures in the Pacific are to be treated with
great caution. "Each new eruption of magma has a
distinctive signature, so different eruptions from
the same place bear different signatures. On the
other hand, the same eruption of magma may surface
in different volcanoes as much as a thousand miles
apart and the obsidians produced will all bear the
same signature. Signature analysis for source of
obsidian works in the Mediterranean area because
there are only three geographical locations for
obsidian there at all and the signatures for each
eruption have been established. For the Pacific,
any conclusions relating to obsidian are entirely
premature. There is, in short, as of now, no evidence of long-distance trade or movement of obsidians in Melanesia" (Ward H. Goodenough, personal communication, February 4, 1974).

5. At Pamua on San Cristobal Island (Map 4),
Green has archaeologically recognized the site
where the Spanish galleon Almiranta landed. This
galleon was part of Mendana's unsuccessful expedition to colonize the Solomons in 1595. A small
occupation site on a hilltop contained Spanish
ceramics and metal tools (Green, 1973).

6. Commander Joseph C. Thompson carried out the
first excavations in Micronesia on Guam in the
Marianas Islands in the early 1920s. This work
was continued by Mr. and Mrs. Hornbostel. Together they recorded hundreds of monuments and recovered potsherds and stone and shell artifacts.
The Hornbostel Collection was studied and reported
by Laura M. Thompson (1932).

References Cited

Abbie, A. A. (1966). "The anthropological status of the Australian Aborigines." Homo, 17: 73-88.

Allen, J. (1972a). "Nebira 4: an early Austronesian site in central Papua." Archaeology and Physical Anthropology in Oceania, 7(2): 92-124.

Allen, J. (1972b). "The first decade in New Guinea archaeology." Antiquity, 46: 180-189.

Allen, J., and R. C. Green (1972). "Mendana 1595 and the fate of the last almiranta: an archaeological investigation." Journal of Pacific History, 7: 73-91.

Ambrose, W. R., and R. C. Green (1972). "First millennium transport of obsidian from New Britain to the Solomon Islands." Nature, 237: 31.

Bayard, D. T. (1966). The Cultural Relationships of the Polynesian Outliers. M.A. thesis, University of Hawaii, Honolulu.

Bellwood, P. (1970). "Dispersal centers in east Polynesia, with special reference to the Society and Marquesas Islands." In R. G. Green and M. Kelly, eds., Studies in Oceanic Culture History, Volume 1. Pacific Anthropological Records,

No. 11. Honolulu: Bernice P. Bishop Museum, Department of Anthropology.

Benedict, P. (1942). "Thai, Kadai, and Indonesian: a new alignment." American Anthropologist, 44: 576-601.

Benedict, P. (1966). "Austro-Thai." Behavior Science Notes, 1: 226-261.

Benedict, P. (1967). "Austro-Thai studies." Behavior Science Notes, 2: 203-244, 275-336.

Beyer, H. O. (1948). Philippine and East Asian Archaeology and Its Relation to the Origin of the Pacific Islands Population. Luzon City: National Research Council of the Philippines, Bulletin 29.

Binford, S., and L. R. Binford (1968). New Perspectives in Archaeology. Chicago: Aldine.

Birdsell, J. B. (1967). "Preliminary data on the trihybrid origin of the Australian Aborigines." Archaeology and Physical Anthropology in Oceania, 2(1): 100-155.

Bordes, F. (1968). The Old Stone Age. World University Library. New York: McGraw-Hill.

Boriskovski, P. T. (1969). "Vietnam in primeval times: part III." Soviet Anthropology and Archaeology, 8(1): 70.

Bowler, J. M., R. Jones, H. Allen, and A. G. Thorne (1970). "Pleistocene human remains from Australia: a living site from Lake Mungo, western New South Wales." World Archaeology, 2(1): 39-60.

Bruijn, J. V. de (1962). "New bronze finds at Kwadeware, Lake Sentani." Nieuw Guinea Studien, 6(1): 61-62.

Bulmer, S. (1964). "Radiocarbon dates from New Guinea." Journal of the Polynesian Society, 73(3): 327-328.

Bulmer, S. (1966). "Pig bone from two archaeologi-
cal sites in the New Guinea highlands." Journal
of the Polynesian Society, 75(4): 504-505.
Bulmer, S., and R. Bulmer (1964). "The prehistory
of the New Guinea highlands." American Anthro-
pologist, 66(4), Part 2.
Capell, A. (1960). Anthropology and Linguistics of
Futuna-Aniwa, New Hebrides. Oceanic Linguistics
Monographs, No. 5. Sydney: University of Sydney.
Capell, A. (1962). "Oceanic linguistics today."
Current Anthropology, 3: 371-396, 422-428.
Chang, K. C. (1969). Fengpitou, Tapenkeng, and
the Prehistory of Taiwan. New Haven: Yale Uni-
versity Publications in Anthropology, No. 73.
Chevalier, L. (1962). "Le problème des Tumuli en
Nouvelle Caledonie." Etudes Melanesiennes, No.
14-17: 24-42.
Chowning, A., and J. C. Goodale (1966). "A flint
industry from southwest New Britain, territory
of New Guinea." Asian Perspectives, 9: 150-153.
Coon, C. S. (1962). The Origin of Races. New
York: Alfred A. Knopf.
Davenport, W. (1968). "Anthropology in the British Solomon Islands." Expedition, Fall: 31-34.
Davenport, W. (1972). "Preliminary excavations
on Santa Ana Island, eastern Solomon Islands."
Archaeology and Physical Anthropology in Oceania,
7(3): 165-183.
Davidson, J. M. (1967). "Preliminary archaeological investigations on Ponape and other eastern
Caroline Islands." Micronesica, 3(2): 82-95.
Davidson, J. M. (1968). "Nukuoro: archaeology on
a Polynesian outlier in Micronesia." In I. Yawata and Y. H. Sinoto, eds., Prehistoric Culture
in Oceania. Honolulu: Bishop Museum Press.
Davidson, J. M. (1969). "Archaeological excavations in two burial mounds at 'Atele, Tongatapu."

Records of the Auckland Institute and Museum,
6(4-6): 251-286.

Davidson, J. M. (1971). "Archaeology on Nukuoro
Atoll, a Polynesian outlier in the eastern Caroline Islands." Auckland: Bulletin of the Auckland Institute and Museum, No. 9.

de Terra, H. (1943). "Pleistocene geology and
early man in Java." Transactions of the American Philosophical Society, 32: 456-457.

Dickinson, W. R. (1971). "Temper sands in Lapita-
style potsherds in Malo." Journal of the Polynesian Society, 80(2): 244-246.

Dortch, C. E., and D. Meirilees (1973). "Human
occupation of Devil's Lair, Western Australia
during the Pleistocene." Archaeology and Physical Anthropology in Oceania, 8(2): 89-115.

Duff, R. (1956). The Moa Hunter Period of Maori
Culture, 2nd ed. Wellington: Canterbury Museum.
Bulletin 1.

Duff, R. (1959). "Neolithic adzes of eastern Poly-
nesia." In J. D. Freeman and W. R. Geddes, eds.,
Anthropology in the South Seas. New Plymouth:
Avery.

Dunn, F. L. (1970). "Cultural evolution in the
late Pleistocene and Holocene of Southeast Asia."
American Anthropologist, 72(5): 1040-1054.

Dyen, I. (1971). "The Austronesian languages and
Proto-Austronesian." In T. A. Sebeok, ed., Current Trends in Linguistics, 8: 5-54.

Egloff, B. J. (1971). Collingwood Bay and the
Trobriand Islands in Recent Prehistory. Unpub-
lished Ph.D. dissertation, Australian National
University, Canberra.

Egloff, B. J. (1972). "The sepulchre pottery of
Nuamata Island, Papua." Archaeology and Physical Anthropology in Oceania, 7(2): 145-163.

Elbert, S. H. (1967). "A linguistic assessment of
the historical validity of some of the Rennel-
lese and Bellonese oral traditions." In G. A.
Highlands, et al., eds., Polynesian Culture History. Special Publication 56. Honolulu: Bernice P. Bishop Museum.

Emory, K. P., and Y. H. Sinoto (1964). "Eastern
Polynesian burials at Maupiti." Journal of the
Polynesian Society, 73(2): 143-160.

Emory, K. P., and Y. H. Sinoto (1969). "Age of the
sites in the South Point area, Ka'u, Hawaii."
Pacific Anthropological Records, No. 8. Honolulu: Bernice P. Bishop Museum, Department of
Anthropology.

Fox, R. B. (1967). "Excavations in the Tabon
caves and some problems in Philippine chronolo-
gy." In M. D. Zamara, ed., Studies in Philippine Anthropology. Luzon City.

Fox, R. B. (1970). The Tabon Caves. Manila:
Monographs of the National Museum, No. 1.

Fox, Robert B., Jesus T. Peralta, Inocentes P.
Paniza, Israel Cabanilla, Ned Ewert, Yogi Aoyagi,
Silvio Lopez, and Rey Flores (1971). "Ancient
Man and Pleistocene Fauna in Cagayan Valley,
Northern Luzon, Philippines: A Progress Report."
Manila: National Museum.

Frimigocci, D. (1970a). "Fouilles archeologiques
a Vatcha (pres de Vao) Ile des Pins." Etudes
Melanesiennes, (n.s.) No. 21-25: 23-42.

Frimigocci, D. (1970b). "Une delation pour la
method du C. 14 du site Lapita de Vatcha (pres
de Vao), Ile des Pins." Etudes Melanesiennes,
(n.s.) No. 21-25: 43-44.

Gallus, A. (1971). "Results of the exploration of
Koonalda Cave 1956-1968." In R. V. S. Wright,
ed., Archaeology of the Gallus Site, Koonalda

Cave. Australian Aboriginal Studies, No. 26.
Canberra: Australian Institute of Aboriginal
Studies.

Garanger, J. (1972). Archeologie des Nouvelles
Hebrides. Paris: Publications de la Societe des
Oceanistes, No. 30, Musée de l'Homme.

Gifford, E. W. (1951). "Archaeological excavations in Fiji." University of California Anthropological Records, 13: 3.

Gifford, E. W., and D. S. Gifford (1959). "Archaeological excavations in Yap." Anthropological Records, 18(2): 149-224.

Gifford, E. W., and D. Shutler, Jr. (1956). "Archaeological excavations in New Caledonia." University of California Anthropological Records,
18: 1.

Glover, I. C. (1971). "Prehistoric research in
Timor." In D. J. Mulvaney and J. Golson, eds.,
Aboriginal Man and Environment in Australia.
Canberra: Australian National University Press.

Golson, J. (1959). "Archeologie du Pacifique sud:
resultats et perspectives." Journal de la So-
cieté des Oceanistes, 15(15): 5-54.

Golson, J. (1962). "Rapport sur les fouilles ef-
fectuées à l'Ile des Pins, Nouvelle-Caledonie,
de Décembre 1959 à Février 1960." Etudes melanesiennes, (n.s.) No. 14-17: 11-23.

Golson, J. (1968). "Archaeological prospects in
Melanesia." In I. Yawata and Y. H. Sinoto, eds.,
Prehistoric Cultures in Oceania. Honolulu:
Bishop Museum Press.

Golson, J. (1971a). "Both sides of the Wallace
Line: Australia, New Guinea, and Asian prehistory." Archaeology and Physical Anthropology
in Oceania, 6(2): 124-144.

Golson, J. (1971b). "Lapita ware and its trans-
formations." In R. C. Green and M. Kelly, eds.,

Studies in Oceanic Culture History, Volume 2.
Pacific Anthropological Records, No. 12.   Honolulu: Bernice P. Bishop Museum.

Golson, J. (1974).   "Archaeology and agricultural
history in the New Guinea highlands."   Canberra:
Australian National University, Department of
Prehistory.

Golson, J., and P. W. Gathercole (1962).   "The
last decade in New Zealand archaeology."
Antiquity, 36(143): 168-174; 36(144): 271-278.

Golson, J., R. J. Lampert, J. M. Wheeler, and W.
R. Ambrose (1967).   "A note on carbon dates for
agriculture in the New Guinea highlands."
Journal of the Polynesian Society, 76: 369-371.

Goodale, J. C. (1966).   "Imlohe and the mysteries
of the Passismanua (Southwest New Britain)."
Expedition, 8(3): 20-31.

Gorman, C. (1971).   "The Hoabinhian and after: subsistence patterns in Southeast Asia during the
late Pleistocene and early Recent periods."
World Archaeology, 2(3): 300-320.

Gould, R. A. (1973).   Australian Archaeology in
Ecological and Ethnographic Perspective.
Andover, Mass.: A Warner Module Publication in
Anthropology, No. 7.

Grace, G. W. (1964).   "Movements of the Malayo-
Polynesians, 1500 B.C.-500 A.D.: the linguistic
evidence."   Current Anthropology, 5: 361-368,
403-404.

Green, R. C. (1963).   "A suggested revision of the
Fijian sequence."   Journal of the Polynesian
Society, 72(3): 235-253.

Green, R. C. (1971).   "Anuta's position in the sub-
grouping of Polynesian languages."   Journal of
the Polynesian Society, 80(3): 355-370.

Green, R. C. (1973a).   "The conquest of the con-
quistadors."   World Archaeology, 5(1): 14-31.

Green, R. C. (1973b). In Auckland Star, July 1.
  Peter Trickett: "Find Alters Theories in Pacif-
  ic."
Green, R. C., and J. M. Davidson, eds. (1969).
  Archaeology in Western Samoa, Volume I. Auck-
  land: Bulletin of the Auckland Institute and
  Museum, No. 6.
Groube, L. M. (1971). "Tonga, Lapita pottery, and
  Polynesian origins." Journal of the Polynesian
  Society, 80(3): 278-316.
Harrisson, T. (1957). "The great cave of Niah: a
  preliminary report on Bornean prehistory." Man,
  57: 161-166.
Harrisson, T. (1959). "New archaeological and
  ethnological results from Niah cave, Sarawak."
  Man, 59: 1-8.
Harrisson, T., and S. J. O'Connor (1969a). Exca-
  vations of the Prehistoric Iron Industry in West
  Borneo, Volume I: Raw Materials and Industrial
  Waste. Data Paper No. 72. Ithaca: Cornell Uni-
  versity, Department of Asian Studies.
Harrisson, T., and S. J. O'Connor (1969b). Exca-
  vations of the Prehistoric Iron Industry in West
  Borneo, Volume II: Associated Artifacts and
  Ideas. Data Paper No. 72. Ithaca: Cornell Uni-
  versity, Department of Asian Studies.
Hedrick, J. D. (1971). "Lapita style pottery from
  Malo Island." Journal of the Polynesian Society,
  80(1): 5-19.
Heekeren, H. R. Van (1957). The Stone Age of In-
  donesia. Verhandelingen van het Koniklijk insti-
  tuut voor taal-, land- en volkenkunde, deel 21.
  The Hague: Martinus Nijhoff.
Heider, K. G. (1960). "A pebble-tool complex in
  Thailand." Asian Perspectives, 11(2): 63-67.
Hendy, C. H., T. A. Rafter, and W. G. Macintosh
  (1972). "The formation of carbonate nodules in

the soils of the Darling Downs, Queensland, Australia, and the dating of the Talgai cranium." Proceedings of the 8th International Conference of Radiocarbon Dating, pp. D106-D126.

Heyerdahl, T. (1952). American Indians in the Pacific. London: Allen and Unwin.

Heyerdahl, T. (1968). Sea Routes to Polynesia. London: Allen and Unwin.

Honolulu Star-Bulletin (1973). September.

Hooijer, D. A. (1950). "Fossil evidence of Austromelanesian migrations in Malaysia." Southwestern Journal of Anthropology, 6(4): 416-422.

Howells, William (1974). The Pacific Islanders. Peoples of the World Series. London: Weidenfeld and Nicolson.

Jacob, T. (1967). Some Problems Pertaining to the Racial History of the Indonesian Region. Utrecht: Privately published.

Jacob, T. (1972). "The absolute date of the Djetis at Modjokerto." Antiquity, 47: 148.

Jennings, J. N. (1971). "Sea level changes and land links." In D. J. Mulvaney and J. Golson, eds., Aboriginal Man and Environment in Australia. Canberra: Australian National University Press.

Jones, R. (1966). "A speculative archaeological sequence for north-west Tasmania." Records of the Queen Victoria Museum, Launceston, 25: 1-13.

Jones, R. (1968). "The geographical background to the arrival of man in Australia and Tasmania." Archaeology and Physical Anthropology in Oceania, 3(3): 186-215.

Keast, A. (1973). Review of Bridge and Banier. "The natural and cultural history of the Torres Strait." In Proceedings of a symposium held in Canberra, Australia, December 1971, D. Walker, ed. Australian Natural University Press.

Keesing, F. M. (1950). "Some notes on early migrations in the Southwest Pacific." Southwestern Journal of Anthropology, 6(2): 101-119.

Kirch, P. V. (1971). "Halawa Dune Site (Hawaiian Islands): a preliminary report." Journal of the Polynesian Society, 80(2): 228-236.

Kirch, P. V., and P. H. Rosendahl (1973). "A note on carbon dates for pottery-bearing layers on Anuta Island." Journal of the Polynesian Society, 82(2): 206-208.

Kirk, R. L. (1971). "Genetic evidence and its implications for aboriginal prehistory." In D. J. Mulvaney and J. Golson, eds., Aboriginal Man and Environment in Australia. Canberra: Australia National University Press.

Lampert, R. J. (1972). "A carbon date for the aboriginal occupation of Kangaroo Island, South Australia." Mankind, 8(3): 223-224.

Lauer, P. K. (1971). "Changing patterns of pottery trade to the Trobriand Islands." World Archaeology, 3(2): 197-209.

Lenormand, M. H. (1948). "Découverte d'une gisement de poteries indigenes à l'Ile des Pins." Etudes Melanesiennes. nes. (n.s.) 3: 54-58.

Macintosh, N. W. G. (1963). "Origin and physical differentiation of the Australian Aborigines." Australia Natural History, 14: 248-252.

Macintosh, N. W. G. (1972). "Radiocarbon dating as a pointer in time to the arrival and history of man in Australia and the islands to the northwest." Proceedings of the 8th International Conference on Radiocarbon Dating, pp. XLIV-LVI.

Macintosh, N. W. G. (1974). "Early man and the dog in Australia." Sir Grafton Elliot Smith Mem. Vol., Sydney University Press.

Macintosh, N. W. G., and S. L. Larnach (1972). "The persistence of Homo Erectus traits in Australian Aboriginal crania." Archaeology and Physical Anthropology in Oceania, 7(1): 1-14.

Macintosh, N. W. G., and S. L. Larnach (1973). "A cranial study of the Aborigines of Queensland with a contrast between Australian and New Guinea crania." In The Human Biology of Aborigines in Cape York. Australian Aboriginal Studies, No. 44. Canberra: Australian Institute of Aboriginal Studies.

Macknight, C. C. (1972). "Macassans and aborigines." Oceania, 42(4): 283-321.

McKern, W. C. (1929). Archaeology of Tonga. Honolulu: Bernice P. Bishop Museum, Bulletin 60.

Meyer, O. (1909). "Funde prähistorischer Töpferei und Steinmesser auf Vatom, Bismarck-Archipel." Anthropos, 4: 251-252, 1093-1095.

Meyer, O. (1910). "Funde von Menchen- und Tierknochen, von prähistorischer Töpferei und Steinwerkzeugen auf Vatom, Bismarck-Archipel." Anthropos, 5: 1160-1161.

Movius, H. L., Jr. (1949). "The Lower Paleolithic cultures of southern and eastern Asia." Transactions of the American Philosophical Society, 38(4): 329-420.

Mulvaney, D. J. (1969). The Prehistory of Australia: Ancient Peoples and Places. London: Thames and Hudson.

Nash, J., and D. D. Mitchell (1973). "A note on some chipped stone objects from south Bougainville." Journal of the Polynesian Society, 82(2): 209-212.

Nielson, E. (1971). "The Thai-Danish Prehistoric Expedition 1960-1962, Preliminary Expedition 1960-1961." Journal of the Siam Society, 49(1): 47-55.

Ollier, C. D., and D. K. Holdsworth (1968). "A
  survey of a megalithic structure in the Tro-
  briand Islands, Papua." Archaeology and Physi-
  cal Anthropology in Oceania, 3(2): 156-158.
Ollier, C. D., D. K. Holdsworth, and G. Heers
  (1970). "Megaliths at Wagoru, Vakuta, Tro-
  briand Islands." Archaeology and Physical
  Anthropology in Oceania, 5(1): 24-26.
Osborne, D. (1966). The Archaeology of the Palau
  Islands. Honolulu: Bernice P. Bishop Museum,
  Bulletin 230.
Palmer, J. B. (1967). "Archaeological sites of
  Wakaya Island." Records of the Fiji Museum,
  1(2): 1-43.
Palmer, J. B. (1969). "Ring-ditch fortifications
  on Windward Viti Levu, Fiji." Archaeology and
  Physical Anthropology in Oceania, 4(3): 181-197.
Paulsen, J. (1967). A Contribution to the Pre-
  history of the Tongan Islands. Unpublished
  Ph.D. dissertation, Australian National Univer-
  sity, Canberra.
Paulsen, J. (1968). "Archaeological excavations
  on Tongatabu." In I. Yawata and Y. H. Sinoto,
  eds., Prehistoric Culture in Oceania. Honolulu:
  Bishop Museum Press.
Pawley, A. (1967). "The relationships of Polyne-
  sian outlier languages." Journal of the Poly-
  nesian Society, 76: 259-296.
Pawley, A. (1972). "On the internal relationships
  of eastern Oceanic languages." In R. G. Green
  and M. Kelly, eds., Studies in Oceanic Culture
  History, Volume 3. Pacific Anthropology Records,
  No. 13. Honolulu: Bernice P. Bishop Museum.
Pearson, R. J., P. V. Kirch, and M. Pietrusewsky
  (1971). "An early prehistoric site at Bellows
  Beach, Warmanalo, Oahu, Hawaiian Islands."
  Archaeology and Physical Anthropology in Oceania,
  6(3): 204-234.

Pellett, M., and A. Spoehr (1961). "Marianas archaeology: report on an excavation on Tinian." Journal of the Polynesian Society, 70(3): 321-325.

Radiocarbon (1965). "Ponape series." American Journal of Sciences, 7: 253-254.

Radiocarbon Dates Association, Inc. (1966). New Haven.

Reinman, F. M. (1968a). "Guam prehistory." In I. Yawata and Y. H. Sinoto, eds., Prehistoric Culture in Oceania. Honolulu: Bishop Museum Press.

Reinman, F. M. (1968b). "Radiocarbon dates from Guam, Marianas Islands." Journal of the Polynesian Society, 77(1): 80-82.

Ross, H. M. (1970). "Stone adzes from Malaita, Solomon Islands: an ethnographic contribution to Melanesian archaeology." Journal of the Polynesian Society, 79(4): 411-420.

Sarasin, F. (1933a). "Recherches prehistoriques au Siam." L'Anthropologie, 42: 1-40.

Sarasin, F. (1933b). "Prehistoric researches in Siam." Journal of the Siam Society, 26(2): 171-202.

Sauer, C. O. (1952). Agricultural Origins and Dispersals. Bowan Memorial Lectures, 2. New York: American Geographical Society.

Saurin, E. (1971). "Les recherches prehistoriques au Combodge, Laos, et Viet Nam (1877-1966)." Asian Perspectives, 12: 27-41.

Semple, N. M., R. T. Simmons, and J. J. Graydon (1956). "Blood group frequencies in natives in the central highlands of New Guinea." Medical Journal of Australia, 2: 365-371.

Sharp, A. (1957). Ancient Voyagers in the Pacific. London: Pelican.

Shaw, E. (1967). "A reanalysis of pottery from
    Navatu and Vunda, Fiji." Unpublished M.A. the-
    sis, University of Auckland.
Shutler, M. E. (1968). "Pottery-making at Wusi,
    New Hebrides." South Pacific Bulletin, 18(4):
    15-18.
Shutler, M. E., and R. Shutler, Jr. (1965). A
    Preliminary Report of Archaeological Explora-
    tions in the Southern New Hebrides, 1963-1964.
    Honolulu: Bernice P. Bishop Museum, Department
    of Anthropology. Spec. Pub.
Shutler, M. E., and R. Shutler, Jr. (1967). "Ori-
    gins of the Melanesians." Archaeology and Phys-
    ical Anthropology in Oceania, 11(2): 91-99.
Shutler, R., Jr. (1971). "Pacific island radio-
    carbon dates: an overview." In R. C. Green and
    M. Kelly, eds., Studies in Oceanic Culture His-
    tory, Volume 2. Pacific Anthropological Records,
    No. 12. Honolulu: Bernice P. Bishop Museum, De-
    partment of Anthropology.
Shutler, R., Jr., and C. A. Kess (1969). A Lithic
    Industry from New Britain, Territory of New
    Guinea, With Possible Areal and Chronological
    Relationships. Bulletin of the Institute of
    Ethnology, Academia Sinica, No. 27.
Shutler, R., Jr., and M. E. Shutler (1965). A
    Preliminary Report of Archaeological Explora-
    tions in the Southern New Hebrides, 1963-1964.
    Photo Offset. Honolulu: Bernice P. Bishop Mu-
    seum.
Shutler, R., Jr., and M. E. Shutler (1968). "Ar-
    chaeological excavations in southern Melanesia."
    In I. Yawata and Y. H. Sinoto, eds., Prehistoric
    Culture in Oceania. Honolulu: Bishop Museum
    Press.
Sieveking, A. (1960). "The Paleolithic industry
    of Kata Tampan, northwestern Malaya." Asian
    Perspectives, 2(2): 91-102.

Simmons, R. T. (1956). "A report on blood group genetical surveys in eastern Asia, Indonesia, Melanesia, Micronesia, Polynesia, and Australia in the study of man." Anthropos, 51: 500-512.

Sinoto, Y. H. (1968). "Position of the Marquesas Islands in east Polynesian prehistory." In I. Yawata and Y. H. Sinoto, eds., Prehistoric Cultures in Oceania. Honolulu: Bishop Museum Press.

Sinoto, Y. H. (1970). "An archaeologically based assessment of the Marquesas as a dispersal center in east Polynesia." In R. C. Green and M. Kelly, eds., Studies in Oceanic Culture History, Volume 1. Pacific Anthropological Records, No. 11. Honolulu: Bernice P. Bishop Museum.

Smith, C. S. (1964). "Archaeological investigations at Pekia, Hiva Oa, Marquesas Islands." Paper read at the Ethnological Congress in Moscow, 1964. Typescript, Department of Anthropology, Bernice P. Bishop Museum, Honolulu.

Soejono, R. P. (1971). "The history of prehistoric research in Indonesia to 1950." Asian Perspectives, 12: 69-91.

Solenberger, R. R. (1967). "The changing role of rice in the Marianas Islands." Micronesia, 3(2): 97-103.

Solheim, W. G., II. (1972). "Early Man in southeast Asia." Expedition, Spring.

Specht, J. (1968). "Preliminary report of excavation on Watom Island." Journal of the Polynesian Society, 77(2): 117-134.

Specht, J. (1969). Prehistoric and Modern Pottery Traditions of Buka Island. Unpublished Ph.D. dissertation, Australian National University, Canberra.

Specht, J. (1972). "Evidence for early trade in northern Melanesia." Mankind, 8(4): 310-312.

Specht, J. (1973). The 1973 Field Season on West
    New Britain and the Huon Peninsula. Typescript,
    Australian Museum, Sydney.
Spicer, E. H., ed. (1961). Perspectives in Ameri-
    can Indian Culture Change. Chicago: University
    of Chicago Press.
Spoehr, A. (1957). "Marianas prehistory: archaeo-
    logical survey and excavations on Saipan, Tinian
    and Rota." Fieldiana Anthropology, 48.
Suggs, R. C. (1961). "Archaeology of Nuku Hiva,
    Marquesas Islands, French Polynesia." American
    Museum of Natural History Anthropological Papers,
    49(1): 1-205.
Suggs, R. C. (1962). "Polynesia Regional report."
    Asian Perspectives, 5(1): 88-94.
Swindler, D. R. (1955). "The absence of the sickle
    gene in several Melanesian societies and its
    anthropologic significance." Human Biology, 27:
    284-293.
Swindler, D. R. (1962). A Racial Study of the West
    Nakanai. Philadelphia: University of Pennsyl-
    vania, The University Museum.
Takayama, J., and T. Egami (1971). Archaeology on
    Rota in the Marianas Islands. Reports of Pacific
    Archaeological Survey, Number 1. Hiratsuka City:
    Tokai University.
Thompson, L. M. (1932). "Archaeology of the Mari-
    anas Islands." Honolulu: Bernice P. Bishop Mu-
    seum, Bulletin 100.
Thorne, A. G. (1971). "The racial affinities and
    origins of the Australian Aborigines." In D. J.
    Mulvaney and J. Golson, eds., Aboriginal Man and
    Environment in Australia. Canberra: Australian
    National University Press.
Thorne, A. G., and P. G. Macumber (1972). "Dis-
    coveries of late Pleistocene man at Kow Swamp,
    Australia." Nature, 238 (5363): 316-319.

Tryon, D. T. (1971). "Linguistic evidence and aboriginal origins." In D. J. Mulvaney and J. Golson, eds., Aboriginal Man and Environment in Australia. Canberra: Australian National University Press.

von Koenigswald, G. H. R. (1936). "Early Paleolithic stone implements from Java." Bulletin of the Raffles Museum, (series B) 1: 52-60.

von Koenigswald, G. H. R. (1960). "Preliminary report on a newly discovered Stone Age culture from northern Luzon, Philippines." Asian Perspectives, 2(2): 70-71.

White, J. P. (1965). "Archaeological excavations in New Guinea: an interim report." Journal of the Polynesian Society, 74(1): 40-56.

White, J. P. (1967). Taim Bilong Bipo: Investigations Towards a Prehistory of the Papua-West New Guinea Highlands. Unpublished Ph.D. dissertation, Australian National University, Canberra.

White, J. P. (1969). "Typologies for some prehistoric flaked stone artifacts of Australian New Guinea Highlands." Archaeology and Physical Anthropology in Oceania, 4(1): 18-46.

White, J. P. (1971). "New Guinea and Australian prehistory: the Neolithic problem." In D. J. Mulvaney and J. Golson, eds., Aboriginal Man and Environment in Australia. Canberra: Australian National University Press.

White, J. P. (1972). "Carbon dates from New Ireland." Mankind, 8(4): 309-310.

White: J. P., K. A. W. Crook, and B. P. Buxton (1970). "Kosipe: a late Pleistocene site in the Papuan Highlands." Proceedings of the Prehistoric Society, 36: 152-170.

White, J. P., and J. Specht (1973). "Prehistoric pottery from Ambitle Island, Bismarck Archipelago." Asian Perspectives, 14: 88-94.

Wright, R. V. S., ed. (1971).   Archaeology of the
   Gallus Site, Koonalda Cave.   Australian Aborig-
   inal Studies, No. 26.   Canberra: Australian In-
   stitute of Aboriginal Studies.
Wurm, S. A. (1967).   "Linguistics and the prehis-
   tory of the Southwestern Pacific."   Journal of
   Pacific History, 2: 25-38.
Yawata, I., and Y. H. Sinoto, eds. (1968).   Pre-
   historic Culture in Oceania.   Honolulu: Bishop
   Museum Press.
Yen, D. (1971).   "The development of agriculture
   in Oceania."   In R. C. Green and M. Kelly, eds.,
   Studies in Oceanic Culture History.   Anthro-
   pological Records, No. 12.   Honolulu: Bernice
   P. Bishop Museum.

Dickinson, W.R., and Richard Shutler, Jr. (1974).
"Probable Fijian Origin of Quartzose Temper Sands
in Prehistoric Pottery from Tonga and the Marquesas."   Science 185: 454-457.

Index

124   Index